Biltmore Estate® SPECIALTIES of the HOUSE

Biltmore Estate
SPECIALTIES
of the HOUSE

Oxmoor House

Library of Congress Catalog Card Number: 94-67754
ISBN: 0-8487-1246-3
Manufactured in the United States of America
First Printing 1994

Editor-in-Chief: Nancy J. Fitzpatrick
Senior Foods Editor: Susan Carlisle Payne
Senior Homes Editor: Mary Kay Culpepper
Senior Editor, Editorial Services: Olivia Kindig Wells
Art Director: James Boone

Biltmore Estate® Specialties of the House

Editor: Cathy A. Wesler
Designer: Alison Turner Bachofer
Copy Editor: Cecilia C. Robinson
Editorial Assistants: Michelle Andrews, Lisa C. Bailey
Contributing Editors: Ginger Crichton, Shannon L. Sexton
Indexer: Mary Ann Laurens
Director, Test Kitchens: Kathleen Royal
Assistant Director, Test Kitchens: Gayle Hays Sadler
Test Kitchen Home Economists: Susan Hall Bellows, Christina A. Crawford, Iris Crawley,
    Michele B. Fuller, Elizabeth Luckett, Kathleen Royal, Angie N. Sinclair, Jan A. Smith
Senior Photographer: Jim Bathie
Senior Photo Stylist: Kay E. Clarke
Illustrator: Kelly Davis
Publishing Systems Administrator: Rick Tucker
Director of Production and Distribution: Phillip Lee
Production Manager: Gail H. Morris
Associate Production Manager: Theresa L. Beste
Production Assistant: Marianne Jordan
Project Manager: Teresa Wilson Lux

Cover: *Turkey Filet Mignon (page 96), Mushroom Ragoût (page 122), Mushroom-Shaped Truffled Potatoes (page 123), Colorful Vegetable Sauté (page 124)*
Back cover: *Marjolaine (page 136)*

$\mathscr{C}$ontents

Foreword

Since the opening of Biltmore House in 1895, guests have enjoyed the hospitality of my grandfather's home in the mountains of North Carolina. In his day, company came to elaborate sixteen-course dinners in the great Banquet Hall, serenaded by orchestral music from the organ loft. They enjoyed more intimate lunches and dinners in the Breakfast Room. And they surely thought it a wonderful treat to take tea on the loggia, surveying the vast panorama of the Blue Ridge before them.

In my time, guests must imagine what life was like at the turn of the century for my grandparents and their family and friends. Theirs is an age that is past, an age the likes of which we will probably never see again. But I have found in spending time with our present-day "company" that their enjoyment of Biltmore is probably no less than that of the company a century ago. A day at Biltmore Estate today is still the foundation of great memories.

In my grandparents' guest register, houseguests would pen heartfelt thanks to their host and hostess for their time at Biltmore Estate, leaving behind poems, sketches, and personal recollections. Their visits were also written about with great fondness in letters afterwards. And just as the guests were grateful for their time at the estate, so my grandparents were pleased to be able to entertain in such a grand style. Back then it was customary for my grandmother to present her parting guests with small favors, nosegays, or personal gifts as a keepsake of their visit. Similarly, over the years many of our current guests have asked for a way to take a little of Biltmore back home with them.

I have wanted to produce a Biltmore Estate cookbook for a long while, not only to satisfy those requests from our guests but also because, quite frankly, little is more fulfilling than my own kitchen. I find great pleasure in creating and preparing a dinner, sharing it with friends and family over good conversation and good wine. The art of gathering around a dinner table and enjoying the company of others is just as rewarding to me now as I'm sure it was to my grandparents 100 years ago. In my opinion it is important for such traditions to continue among families and friends.

With this hope, *Biltmore Estate® Specialties of the House* is presented—to fill your table with memorable gatherings of people with whom you enjoy spending time and making conversation. Each time you use it, may your home be full of the same spirit of graciousness that has enlivened and continues to help preserve Biltmore House as it enters its second century. Enjoy and *bon appetit*!

WILLIAM AMHERST VANDERBILT CECIL

100 Years

of

Biltmore Estate®

*From Victorian times to the present, Biltmore Estate
has entertained visitors with its magnificent setting, an abundance
of activities, and the finest of foods and wines.*

When George Washington Vanderbilt III decided to create Biltmore Estate, he was inspired by the grand country homes he had visited in Europe. He wanted a place in the rolling mountains of North Carolina where he could invite family and friends to the same kind of lavish house parties he had enjoyed abroad. Biltmore Estate, with its 250-room French Renaissance mansion and 125,000 acres of gardens, fields, and forest, was to become the setting for Victorian entertainment at its finest.

Year-Round Festivities

Carriage parade, 1906

The first big party held in Biltmore House was at Christmas, 1895, when most of the construction on the mansion had been completed. Over the next thirty years the estate hosted holiday gatherings, May Day celebrations, elegant picnics, and other grand affairs, such as springtime parades of carriages gaily decorated with flowers. In 1924 perhaps the most spectacular event of all took place—the wedding of Cornelia Vanderbilt, the only child of George and his wife, Edith. The festivities included a wedding luncheon for a thousand guests, among them "notables from all parts of the world," the *New York Times* reported.

Biltmore House was not a full-time residence for the Vanderbilts, who owned homes elsewhere in the country as well as an apartment in Paris. But George Vanderbilt wanted Biltmore House to be a showcase for his fine art and book collections, while being a self-sufficient, working country estate.

Whenever the Vanderbilts returned to Biltmore Estate, they delighted in entertaining their guests in such a spectacular setting. Often visitors stayed for weeks at a time, and Biltmore Estate, which was designed with a wealth of indoor and outdoor recreation opportunities, was perfectly suited to this Victorian custom.

From Croquet to Charades

Outdoor activities at Biltmore Estate included horseback riding, hunting, croquet, fishing, archery, and tennis. Meticulously groomed gardens provided a scenic backdrop for strolling. Indoors, recreation focused on Victorian parlor games, perhaps charades or tableaux vivants (still-life scenes with costumes and explanatory music); card games such as whist; and board games, including chess. Female guests gathered in the ornate Morning Salon to sip tea or pen letters. The men, meanwhile, slipped off to relax in their own retreat—the oak-paneled Billiard Room or the adjoining Smoking Room and Gun Room.

Biltmore House's basement provided still more amusements: a bowling alley, a gymnasium, a swimming pool, and seventeen dressing rooms. Because each activity had its own dress code, a nineteenth-century lady might have changed her clothes five or more times a day.

Spotlight on Food

Besides these recreations, guests' visits were highlighted with such special events as fancy dinners, tea dances, costume parties, and balls. And whether they were formal dinners or family luncheons, meals were usually elaborate. A handwritten Biltmore Estate menu dated March 26, 1896, lists the following:

> *Blue Points*
> *celery olives radishes*
> *salted almonds*
> *Saucie de Lyons*
> *Consumme Royale*
> *Parisienne Potatoes*
> *Cucumber Salad*
> *Terrapin ala Maryland*
> *Sweetbreads with*
> *French Peas*
> *Sorbet*
> *Lettuce Salad*
> *Cheese & Biscuits*
> *Ice Cream*
> *Fruit & Coffee*

A Cherished Cookbook

The Encyclopædia of Practical Cookery is part of Biltmore Estate's collection of over 22,000 books. We've updated a few of its recipes to today's cooking methods and placed them throughout this book. These recipes are identified with the symbol at the top of this box. Sample recipes in their original form follow.

FIG. 263. DAUPHIN CAKE

DAUPHIN CAKE — Beat well together in a basin 1lb. of butter and the yolks of sixteen eggs, place over the fire, stirring so as to thicken without taking colour. Remove and let it cool, then add sixteen more yolks and 1lb. of sugar. Work the whole well with a spoon so as to make it light. Then add a little salt and the grated zest of a lemon or orange. Take sixteen of the whites of the eggs, and when whipped add to the mixture with 1 tablespoonful of potato-flour. Pour it out on to a baking-sheet to about 1¼ in. in thickness, cover with buttered paper, and bake in a moderate oven. When it is cool, cut it up into round flats, graduated so as to fill up the dome, raising these flats on a dish the same as a Neapolitan Cake, and mask each one with apricot marmalade. Cover the surface with a layer of meringue, and ornament it with the cornet (see Fig. 263). Sprinkle a little sugar over the part ornamented, and put it in a moderate oven to get a little browned; then take it out, and garnish the cavities of the decoration with preserved cherries. Apricot sauce must be served up separately.

FIG. 289. RISCASOLI CAKE

RISCASOLI CAKE — The following receipt is given by Dubois for the preparation of this Cake: Mix together ¾ lb. of wheat- and potato-flour in equal parts, 1lb. of caster sugar, 5oz. of butter warmed to melting, the yolks of six eggs, a little salt, and vanilla or any other flavouring to taste. Make it into a dough with milk, but work in the butter after the whites of eggs. Fill a buttered dome-shaped mould well dusted with potato-flour with this. Bake in a moderate oven. When turned out and cooled, cut it horizontally into slices about ½ in. thick, then rebuild the Cake into its original form, putting one slice on top of another, soaking each of them with a little alkermes liqueur. Mask them also one by one on the top with a layer of vanilla-flavoured frangipane, and finish with alkermes liqueur. Place the Cake on a cold dish, mask the surface first with a thin layer of apricot marmalade or greengage marmalade, then with a layer of whipped cream, sweetened, flavoured, and kept very firm. Smooth the surfaces well, decorate them with the same cream, squeezed through a cornet, as shown in Fig. 289, garnish with a ring of macaroons, and serve as soon as ready.

The occasion for the menu is unknown, but guests at the time were George Vanderbilt's sisters Lila Vanderbilt and Margaret Shepard; Edith Shepard, George Vanderbilt's niece; and Virginia Bacon, his aunt.

Fine wine was an important accompaniment to any Biltmore Estate gathering. Victorians realized that good wine stimulates taste and enhances the flavor of food. So at dinners a different wine, chosen carefully to complement the food, was served with each course. Biltmore Estate archives contain receipts for cases of wine that George Vanderbilt bought during his many travels throughout Europe.

Other alcoholic beverages also were available at various affairs through the day. For instance, a December 30, 1893, Biltmore Estate receipt from The Bonanza Wine & Liquor Co. in Asheville, North Carolina, shows purchases of beer, sherry, rye whisky, rum, and California brandy.

Guests of Honor

The Vanderbilts' hospitality was enjoyed by guests from distinguished social, political, and art circles. Some of the more notable visitors were Isabella Stewart Gardner, an art collector and social leader; Don Juan Riano y Gayangos, Spanish ambassador to the United States; Ogden Codman, Jr., an architect and interior designer; Anna Roosevelt Cowles, sister of Teddy Roosevelt; Esme William Howard, British ambassador to the United States; and authors Henry James, Edith Wharton, and Paul Leicester Ford.

In 1899, Ford, who visited Biltmore Estate several times, dedicated one of his books to his close friend George Vanderbilt. Ford wrote of his fond memories of "Mt. Pisgah and the French Broad River, or the ramp and the terrace of Biltmore House . . . our games of chess, our cups of tea, our walks, our rides, and our drives."

A dinner table in Pompadour style, *The Encyclopædia of Practical Cookery*

The Christmas Spirit

Biltmore Estate Christmas celebrations captivated Edith Wharton. On one holiday visit, she wrote to a friend: "We had a big Christmas fete for the 350 people on the estate—a tree 30 ft. high, Punch and Judy [a puppet show], conjuror, presents and 'refreshments.' It would have interested you, it was done so well and sympathetically, each person's wants being thought of, from mother to last baby."

Christmas was indeed a magical time at Biltmore Estate, and the mansion likely was decorated with trees, topiaries, and evergreen roping, as well as elaborate glass ornaments, ribbons, dried flowers, berries, and candles. The 350 people whom Edith Wharton mentioned included Biltmore Estate employees and their families, since the Vanderbilts invited the families of Estate workers to the house each year for a Christmas party. The children of the workers all received gifts (a tradition that continues today) that were wrapped in boxes and hung on a tremendous tree in the Banquet Hall. The annual party reflected the good relationship between the Vanderbilts and the employees—butlers, cooks, maids, stablehands, and so on—needed to run the huge estate. About eighty servants worked in the house and stable area.

May Days and Picnics

While the Christmas holidays were certainly notable, springtime also brought lively festivities and celebrations to Biltmore Estate. At the turn of the century, May Day was considered the spring version of the Thanksgiving harvest festival. Archival photographs show the traditional May Day dance performed by young girls winding long, brightly colored ribbons around a tall Maypole in a field near the Lodge Gate. May Day was also a time to indulge in the Victorian passion for floral decorations. The dining table might have been made to look like a garden, with beds of colorful food artfully set among flowers and vines.

The warm days of spring and summer also gave the Vanderbilt guests a chance to venture from the house for sumptuous country picnics. These were no simple basket-and-blanket affairs. Guests traveled by horse-drawn carriages to a beautiful setting, and servants brought along silver tableware, fine china, and plenty of food. A picnic menu might have included such fare as soup, chicken salad, cold cuts, cheese, crackers, sandwiches of lobster mayonnaise or veal loaf, sherbet, and sponge cake.

Victorian picnickers played at games such as croquet or lawn bowling, or might have fished or strolled nearby. And there was no shortage of drinks. *Mrs. Beeton's Book of Household Management,* published in 1861, suggested for a picnic of forty people "three dozen quarts of ale, packed in hampers; ginger beer, soda water and lemonade, of each two dozen bottles; six bottles of sherry, six bottles of claret, champagne a discretion, and other light wine that may be preferred . . . ."

Setting the Scene

When guests dined inside Biltmore House, they usually enjoyed large formal dinners held in the magnificent medieval-style Banquet Hall, with its ceiling arching 70 feet above a room 72 feet long and 42 feet wide. An enormous stone triple fireplace, topped by the Vanderbilt crest, is at one end of the room, and five sixteenth-century tapestries hang on the walls. The acoustics of this room are said to be so perfect that people sitting at opposite ends of the long table did not have to raise their voices to address each other.

For less formal dining, guests were served in the smaller distinctive Family Dining Room, with its unusual blue jasperware fireplace mantel and walls of Spanish leather.

A Wedding to Remember

In 1924, ten years after George Vanderbilt's sudden death at age fifty-one, Biltmore Estate was the scene of lavish wedding festivities held for his daughter, Cornelia Vanderbilt, and

A Winter Garden Salad Sampler (page 36). The Winter Garden is furnished exactly as it was during the Vanderbilts' time at Biltmore House. The most lavish event to occur in this room was the reception following Cornelia Vanderbilt's wedding to The Honorable John Francis Amherst Cecil in 1924. This indoor conservatory was filled with flowers freshly picked from the Estate grounds, and the table was set with the finest silver and china of the era.

Afternoon Tea in the Library (page 42). It takes only one step into the Library to appreciate Biltmore Estate's vast book collection. The room itself houses over 10,000 volumes, while the entire book collection numbers over 22,000. Reflecting Mr. Vanderbilt's broad interests, the shelves are laden with literary classics as well as works on art, history, architecture, and landscape gardening.

Dinner in the Family Dining Room (page 46). The Family Dining Room, also known as the Breakfast Room, was used for more informal, intimate dining than the Banquet Hall. Today, as in those days, family portraits adorn the Spanish leather walls, instilling the importance of ancestry. Fine silver was always part of this table setting. Before the 1800s, silver was possessed primarily by royalty and the Church. But by the time of his death in 1914, Mr. Vanderbilt had assembled the vast collection that is now the Biltmore Estate silver collection, all original pieces, containing an array of unique selections, in addition to table service. Menu cards, another elegant touch to the table, were commonplace; hand-lettered and located at each place setting, the cards were given to guests as keepsakes of the occasion.

Appetizer Buffet in the Tapestry Gallery (page 52). Ornate tapestries, decorated fireplaces, and a stenciled ceiling incorporate the Gothic period into the Tapestry Gallery. This room would have been a wonderful place for hosting dances and entertaining guests. With the doors to the Loggia open, guests could stroll out to the balcony for a breathtaking view of the Blue Ridge Mountains.

The Encyclopædia of Practical Cookery is a Victorian cookbook from the Biltmore Estate collection. Throughout our chapters you'll find recipes updated from these books, and we've designated each with the Vanderbilt symbol.

Deerpark Restaurant continues to share the Victorian heritage of fine food and drink. Since its opening in 1979, guests have requested favorite recipes from the chef. Each of these recipe treasures bears the acorns and oak leaf symbol.

Celebration Dinner in the Banquet Hall

Caviar Mousse

Pear and Goat Cheese Salad
With Dijon Dressing

Biltmore Estate Sauvignon Blanc

———

Pork Tenderloin Roasted in Rock Salt

Pecan-Wild Rice Pilaf

Green Beans Parmesan

Orange Biscuits

Chateau Biltmore Merlot or
Biltmore Estate Cardinal's Crest

———

Mocha-Pecan Torte

Sparkling Fruit Compotes

Raspberry Mousse in Chocolate Baskets

Serves 24

Caviar Mousse

2	packages unflavored gelatin
½	cup lemon juice
12	hard-cooked eggs, sieved
2¼	cups mayonnaise
1½	teaspoons white wine Worcestershire sauce
¾	teaspoon hot sauce
3	(2-ounce) jars red caviar, drained

Lightly oil a 5½-cup mold; place in freezer 30 minutes. Sprinkle gelatin over lemon juice in top of a double boiler; let stand 1 minute. Bring water to a boil; reduce heat to low, and cook until gelatin dissolves. Remove from heat; add eggs and next 3 ingredients, stirring well. Spoon three-fourths of egg mixture into prepared mold, spreading to fill sides of mold and leaving a well through center of mixture. Freeze 10 minutes. Combine remaining one-fourth of egg mixture and caviar. Remove mold from freezer; pour caviar mixture into well. Chill at least 8 hours. Unmold and serve with crackers. Yield: 5½ cups.

Pear and Goat Cheese Salad with Dijon Dressing

1½	cups olive oil
1½	tablespoons dried whole basil
1½	tablespoons chopped fresh chives
8	(3.5-ounce) logs Sonoma or Montrachet goat cheese
¾	cup white wine vinegar
¼	cup finely chopped green onions
3	tablespoons finely chopped fresh parsley
2½	tablespoons Dijon mustard
¾	teaspoon salt
¾	teaspoon black pepper
2	cups walnut oil
1½	cups soft breadcrumbs, toasted
8	cups torn Bibb lettuce
8	cups torn radicchio
8	cups torn romaine lettuce
4	(16-ounce) cans pear halves, drained and diced
2	medium-size green peppers, seeded and diced
1½	cups chopped walnuts

Combine first 3 ingredients in a shallow dish. Slice cheese into 48 rounds; place in olive oil mixture. Cover; chill at least 6 hours. Combine vinegar and next 5 ingredients in a bowl; gradually add walnut oil in a slow, steady stream, beating with a wire whisk. Cover dressing; chill. Drain cheese. Coat slices with breadcrumbs; place on baking sheets. Bake at 400° for 10 minutes or until lightly browned. Cool. Combine lettuce; place with cheese on salad plates. Sprinkle with pear, green pepper, and walnuts. Drizzle dressing over each serving. Yield: 24 servings.

Pork Tenderloin Roasted in Rock Salt

1	(4-pound) package rock salt
1	cup Riesling
5	(1½-pound) pork tenderloins
⅓	cup chopped fresh rosemary
1	tablespoon freshly ground pepper

Place a large sheet of heavy-duty aluminum foil on a large jellyroll pan. Spread rock salt over aluminum foil; sprinkle Riesling over rock salt until moistened. Sprinkle tenderloins with rosemary and pepper. Roll tenderloins in rock salt, pressing firmly, until rock salt adheres to tenderloins. Bring sides of foil up and around sides of tenderloins, partially sealing foil.

Bake at 500° for 40 to 45 minutes or until meat thermometer inserted into thickest part of tenderloins registers 160°. Let stand 10 minutes. Remove and discard rock salt. Slice tenderloins, and place on a serving platter. Yield: 24 servings.

Pecan-Wild Rice Pilaf

5	cups chicken broth
2	cups wild rice, uncooked
6⅔	cups water
4	(6-ounce) packages wheat pilaf mix
2	cups chopped pecans, toasted
2	cups currants
1½	cups thinly sliced green onions
1	cup chopped fresh parsley
½	cup chopped fresh mint
3	tablespoons grated orange rind
¼	cup orange juice
3	tablespoons olive oil
½	teaspoon freshly ground pepper
2	(11-ounce) cans mandarin oranges, drained

Bring chicken broth to a boil in a Dutch oven; stir in wild rice. Cover, reduce heat, and simmer 50 to 60 minutes or until rice is tender and liquid is absorbed. Set aside, and keep warm.

Bring water to a boil in a large saucepan; stir in wheat pilaf mix and seasoning packets from mix. Cover, reduce heat, and simmer 15 minutes or until wheat pilaf is tender and liquid is absorbed. Combine wild rice, wheat pilaf, pecans, and remaining ingredients in a large bowl; stir well. Yield: 24 servings.

Green Beans Parmesan

4	pounds fresh young green beans
2½	cups diced sweet yellow pepper
2	cups diced sweet red pepper
⅔	cup chopped onion
3	cloves garlic, minced
¼	cup vegetable oil
3	tablespoons chopped fresh basil
1	tablespoon chopped fresh oregano
1	tablespoon chopped fresh thyme
½	teaspoon black pepper
1¾	cups freshly grated Parmesan cheese, divided

Wash beans; trim ends, and remove strings. Cook beans in boiling water to cover 5 minutes; drain. Cook sweet peppers, onion, and garlic in hot oil 3 minutes in a large skillet. Add beans, basil, and next 3 ingredients; cover and simmer 10 minutes or until tender. Stir in 1¼ cups cheese. Transfer to a serving dish; sprinkle with remaining ½ cup cheese. Yield: 24 servings.

Orange Biscuits

1	package active dry yeast
½	cup warm water (105° to 115°)
1	cup warm milk (105° to 115°)
¾	cup sugar
¼	cup butter or margarine, melted
2	egg yolks, beaten
½	cup chopped almonds
2	teaspoons grated orange rind
½	teaspoon salt
5 to 5½	cups all-purpose flour
1	large egg, lightly beaten
1	tablespoon water

Combine yeast and warm water in a 1-cup liquid measuring cup; let stand 5 minutes. Combine yeast mixture, warm milk, and next 3 ingredients in a mixing bowl; beat at medium speed of an electric mixer until well blended. Stir in almonds, orange rind, and salt. Gradually stir in enough flour to make a soft dough. Turn dough out onto a well-floured surface, and knead 1 minute. Place in a well-greased bowl, turning to grease top. Cover and let rise in a warm place (85°), free from drafts, 1 hour or until doubled in bulk.

Punch dough down, and divide into fourths; shape each portion into 6 (3-inch) balls. Roll each ball into a 9-inch rope. Carefully tie each rope into a loose knot. Place 2 inches apart on greased baking sheets. Cover and let rise in a warm place, free from drafts, 45 minutes or until doubled in bulk. Combine egg and 1 tablespoon water; brush over tops of biscuits. Bake at 400° for 15 minutes or until golden. Yield: 2 dozen.

Mocha-Pecan Torte

8	eggs, separated
⅔	cup sifted powdered sugar
1	teaspoon baking powder
⅓	cup cocoa
⅓	cup soft breadcrumbs
1	teaspoon vanilla extract
2	cups ground pecans
2½	teaspoons instant coffee granules
2	tablespoons water
¾	cup plus 2 tablespoons butter, softened
1	tablespoon plus 2 teaspoons cocoa
7	cups sifted powdered sugar
⅓	cup half-and-half
1	teaspoon vanilla extract
	Chocolate candy sprinkles

Line the bottom of 4 (8-inch) round cakepans with wax paper. Grease and flour wax paper; set pans aside.

Combine egg yolks, ⅔ cup powdered sugar, and baking powder in a large bowl; beat at high speed of an electric mixer 2 to 3 minutes or until mixture is thick and pale. Combine ⅓ cup cocoa and breadcrumbs; stir into egg yolk mixture. Stir in 1 teaspoon vanilla; fold in ground pecans.

Beat egg whites in a large bowl until stiff peaks form; gently fold one-fourth of egg whites into yolk mixture. Fold remaining egg whites into yolk mixture. Pour batter evenly into prepared pans; spread top of batter to smooth. Bake at 350° for 15 minutes or until layers spring back when lightly touched. (Do not overbake.) Cool in pans 5 minutes. Invert layers onto wire racks, and gently peel off wax paper. (Layers will be thin.) Cool completely.

Dissolve coffee granules in water; set aside. Beat butter at medium speed of an electric mixer until creamy. Add coffee mixture and 1 tablespoon plus 2 teaspoons cocoa; beat well. Gradually add 7 cups powdered sugar alternately with half-and-half, beating until light and fluffy. Stir in 1 teaspoon vanilla. Set aside 1½ cups frosting for piping. Spread remaining frosting between layers and on top and sides of torte. Gently pat chocolate sprinkles onto sides of torte. Lightly score frosting on top of torte into 12 wedges. Spoon reserved frosting into a large decorating bag fitted with metal tip No. 2F. Pipe 12 rosettes of frosting evenly around top edge of torte; sprinkle rosettes with chocolate sprinkles. Pipe frosting around bottom edge of torte. Chill thoroughly. Yield: one 8-inch torte.

Sparkling Fruit Compotes

    2   cups cantaloupe balls
    2   cups honeydew balls
    2   cups peeled, cored, and cubed fresh pineapple
    2   cups medium-size fresh strawberries
    ½   cup dry white wine
    ½   cup Grand Marnier or other orange-flavored liqueur
    ¼   cup sugar
    2   cups peeled, sliced kiwifruit (about 6 large)
    2   cups fresh blackberries
    1½ cups champagne, divided

Combine first 4 ingredients in a bowl. Combine wine, liqueur, and sugar; stir until sugar dissolves. Pour over fruit; cover and chill at least 3 hours. Add kiwifruit and blackberries. Spoon into individual compotes. Pour 2 tablespoons champagne over each. Yield: 12 servings.

Raspberry Mousse in Chocolate Baskets

    4   (10-ounce) packages frozen raspberries, thawed
    1   tablespoon plus 2 teaspoons unflavored gelatin
    ⅔   cup orange juice
    ½   cup sugar
    ¼   cup Grand Marnier or other orange-flavored liqueur
    28 (1-ounce) squares semisweet chocolate
    4   cups whipping cream, whipped
        Garnishes: fresh raspberries, fresh mint sprigs

Drain raspberries, reserving 2 cups juice; set juice aside. Position knife blade in food processor bowl; add raspberries. Process until smooth; transfer to a wire-mesh strainer. Press with back of spoon against sides of strainer to squeeze out juice. Discard pulp and seeds remaining in strainer.

Sprinkle gelatin over orange juice in a saucepan; let stand 1 minute. Add raspberry juice, puree, and sugar; cook over low heat, stirring until gelatin and sugar dissolve, about 2 minutes. Remove from heat; let cool. Stir in liqueur; chill until consistency of unbeaten egg white.

Place 12 (6-ounce) custard cups upside down on baking sheets. Mold aluminum foil firmly over each custard cup, allowing the foil to extend 1 to 2 inches from the bottom of each cup. Press foil tightly around the bottom of each cup, making a definite edge; chill.

Place chocolate in top of a double boiler; bring water to a boil. Reduce heat to low; cook until chocolate melts, stirring occasionally. Remove from heat; let stand 10 minutes or until thick enough to pipe. Spoon half of chocolate into a decorating bag fitted with a round metal tip. Drizzle chocolate in a lacy design over each custard cup. Chill baskets 5 minutes or until chocolate is firm. Repeat drizzling procedure with remaining melted chocolate. Chill baskets 20 minutes or until firm. Gently peel foil away from baskets. (Baskets may be stored in an airtight container in the refrigerator or freezer.) Gently fold whipped cream into raspberry mixture. Chill 30 minutes or until almost set. Spoon into chocolate baskets; chill until mixture is set. Garnish, if desired. Yield: 12 servings.

Mocha-Pecan Torte (page 23), Raspberry Mousse in
Chocolate Baskets, Sparkling Fruit Compotes

Holiday Breakfast in Mrs. Vanderbilt's Bedroom

Country Garden Omelets
or
Creamy Egg Scramble

Miniature Sausage Muffins

Honey Butter

Marmalade Pears

Biltmore Estate "Brut" Champagne

Hot Tea

Serves 2

Country Garden Omelets

½   cup chopped green pepper
⅓   cup chopped green onions
2   tablespoons sliced pimiento
1   tablespoon butter or margarine, melted
¼   teaspoon dried basil
4   large eggs, separated
2   tablespoons water, divided
¼   teaspoon salt, divided
⅛   teaspoon ground white pepper, divided
2   tablespoons butter or margarine, divided
     Garnish: fresh basil sprigs

Cook first 3 ingredients in 1 tablespoon butter in a medium skillet over medium heat, stirring constantly, until tender; sprinkle with dried basil. Set vegetable mixture aside, and keep warm.

Beat 2 egg yolks in a small bowl until thick and pale. Beat 2 egg whites at high speed of an electric mixer until foamy; add 1 tablespoon water, ⅛ teaspoon salt, and dash of white pepper. Beat until stiff peaks form; gently fold whites into yolks.

Place an 8-inch ovenproof skillet over medium heat until hot. Add 1 tablespoon butter, rotating pan to coat bottom. Spread egg mixture in pan. Cook, uncovered, 2 minutes or until lightly browned. Bake at 325° for 2 to 5 minutes or until a knife inserted in center comes out clean. Loosen omelet with a spatula.

Spoon 2 tablespoons vegetable mixture over half of omelet; fold omelet in half, and gently slide onto a serving plate. Keep warm. Repeat procedure with remaining ingredients for additional omelet. Garnish, if desired. Yield: 2 servings.

Creamy Egg Scramble

3   eggs
¼   cup milk
½   (3-ounce) package cream cheese, cubed
⅛   teaspoon salt
     Dash of pepper
3   tablespoons chopped green onions
1½   tablespoons butter or margarine

Combine first 5 ingredients in container of an electric blender; cover and process at medium speed until frothy (7 to 10 seconds). Stir in onions.

Melt butter in a large nonstick skillet over medium heat, tilting pan to coat bottom; pour in egg mixture. Cook without stirring until mixture begins to set on bottom. Draw a spatula across bottom of pan to form large curds. Continue cooking until eggs are thickened, but still moist; do not stir constantly. Yield: 2 servings.

Miniature Sausage Muffins

¼ pound ground pork sausage
3 tablespoons chopped onions
¾ cup biscuit mix
¼ teaspoon dry mustard
⅛ teaspoon ground red pepper
¼ cup milk
¼ cup (1 ounce) finely shredded Cheddar cheese

Combine sausage and onions in a medium skillet; cook over medium heat, stirring until sausage crumbles. Drain well.

Combine biscuit mix, dry mustard, and red pepper; add milk, stirring just until moistened. Stir in sausage mixture and cheese (mixture will be thick). Spoon into greased miniature (1¾-inch) muffin pans, filling two-thirds full. Bake at 400° for 12 to 14 minutes or until muffins are golden. Remove from pans immediately; serve warm. Yield: 1 dozen.

Honey Butter

¼ cup plus 2 tablespoons butter, softened
⅔ cup honey
½ teaspoon grated lemon rind

Beat butter at medium speed of an electric mixer until creamy; gradually add honey, beating well. Add lemon rind; beat well. Cover and chill. Serve with muffins or toast. Yield: 1 cup.

Marmalade Pears

2½ tablespoons orange marmalade
2 tablespoons orange juice
1 (16-ounce) can pear halves, drained

Combine all ingredients in a large skillet. Cover and cook over medium heat until thoroughly heated, stirring gently. Spoon pears and juice mixture into individual serving bowls. Yield: 2 to 3 servings.

Picnic in the Azalea Garden

Stuffed Celery Sticks

Fruited Chicken Salad

Curried Rice Salad

Pickled Peaches

Cheese Biscuits

Mint Tea

Biltmore Estate Chardonnay sur Lies

Spiced Shortbread Cookies

Serves 6

Stuffed Celery Sticks

1   (3-ounce) package cream cheese, softened
⅓   cup finely chopped pecans, toasted
2   tablespoons mayonnaise
1   tablespoon dried parsley flakes
¼   teaspoon Beau Monde seasoning
⅛   teaspoon garlic powder
4   celery stalks, cut into 3-inch pieces

Combine cream cheese, chopped pecans, mayonnaise, parsley flakes, seasoning, and garlic powder; mix well. Pipe or spread cream cheese mixture evenly onto celery pieces. Cover and chill at least 4 hours. Yield: 1 dozen.

Fruited Chicken Salad

2¼ cups diced cooked chicken
3   tablespoons thinly sliced celery
3   tablespoons chopped green pepper
2   green onions, chopped
1   tablespoon lemon juice
¾   cup halved seedless green grapes
1   (11-ounce) can mandarin oranges in light syrup, drained
⅓   cup mayonnaise
3   tablespoons coarsely chopped pecans, toasted
¼   teaspoon salt
⅛   teaspoon pepper
    Lettuce leaves

Combine first 5 ingredients in a large bowl, and toss gently. Cover and chill. Add grapes and next 5 ingredients; toss well. Arrange salad evenly on individual lettuce-lined plates. Yield: 6 servings.

Curried Rice Salad

1   (6-ounce) package long-grain and wild rice mix
2   cups chicken broth
1   cup raisins
1   cup hot water
1   (15-ounce) can garbanzo beans, drained
1   cup chopped pecans, toasted
½   cup sliced green onions
    Curry Dressing
    Lettuce leaves

Combine rice mix, seasoning packet from mix, and broth in a saucepan. Bring to a boil; cover, reduce heat, and simmer 20 to 25 minutes or until rice is tender and liquid is absorbed. Remove from heat, and let cool.

Combine raisins and water; let stand 10 minutes. Drain. Stir raisins, beans, and next 3 ingredients into rice mixture; cover and chill. Serve on lettuce leaves. Yield: 6 to 8 servings.

Curry Dressing

⅔　cup mayonnaise
1　tablespoon curry powder
1　tablespoon honey
1　tablespoon vinegar
2　teaspoons prepared mustard
1　teaspoon Worcestershire sauce
⅛　teaspoon ground red pepper

Combine all ingredients; cover and chill. Yield: ¾ cup.

Pickled Peaches

3　quarts cold water
¾　teaspoon ascorbic-citric powder
8　pounds small to medium-size firm, ripe peaches, peeled
6¾　cups sugar
1　quart vinegar (5% acidity)
4　(3-inch) sticks cinnamon
2　tablespoons whole cloves
3　pieces whole mace

Combine water and ascorbic-citric powder in a large container. Place peaches in water mixture; set aside.

Combine sugar and vinegar in a large Dutch oven; bring to a boil, and cook 5 minutes. Place cinnamon, cloves, and mace on a piece of cheesecloth; tie ends of cheesecloth securely. Add to syrup mixture.

Drain peaches, and add to syrup mixture. Cook, uncovered, over medium heat 3 minutes or just until peaches can be pierced with a fork. Remove from heat. Cover and let stand at room temperature 24 hours.

Bring peaches to a boil; pack hot peaches into hot jars, leaving ½-inch headspace. Pour boiling syrup over peaches, leaving ½-inch headspace. Remove air bubbles; wipe jar rims. Cover at once with metal lids, and screw on bands. Process in boiling-water bath 20 minutes. Yield: 6 pints.

Cheese Biscuits

1   cup all-purpose flour
1½   teaspoons baking powder
⅛   teaspoon salt
¼   cup shortening
½   cup (2 ounces) shredded sharp Cheddar cheese
¼   cup milk

Combine first 3 ingredients in a bowl; cut in shortening and cheese with pastry blender. Add milk; stir with a fork until dry ingredients are moistened. Turn dough out onto a lightly floured surface; knead 3 or 4 times. Roll to ½-inch thickness; cut with a 2¼-inch round cutter. Place on a greased baking sheet. Bake at 450° for 10 minutes or until golden. Yield: 8 biscuits.

Mint Tea

1   quart boiling water
2   quart-size tea bags
¾   cup packed fresh mint leaves
1   cup sugar
¼   cup plus 2 tablespoons fresh lemon juice
1   quart cold water
        Garnish: fresh mint sprigs

Pour boiling water over tea bags and ¾ cup mint leaves in a teapot or saucepan; cover and steep 5 to 10 minutes. Remove and discard tea bags and mint. Add sugar and lemon juice, stirring until sugar dissolves. Stir in cold water. Serve over ice. Garnish, if desired. Yield: 2 quarts.

Spiced Shortbread Cookies

1   cup butter or margarine, softened
⅔   cup sifted powdered sugar
½   teaspoon ground nutmeg
½   teaspoon ground cinnamon
½   teaspoon ground ginger
2   cups all-purpose flour

Beat butter at medium speed of an electric mixer until creamy; gradually add sugar, beating well. Add spices, and beat well. Stir in flour. (Dough will be stiff.) Shape dough into 1¼-inch balls; place 2 inches apart on lightly greased cookie sheets. Lightly press cookies with a floured cookie stamp or fork to flatten to ¼-inch thickness. Bake at 325° for 15 to 18 minutes or until lightly browned. Remove to wire racks to cool. Yield: 2½ dozen.

Curried Rice Salad (page 32), Pickled Peaches (page 33), Stuffed Celery Sticks
(page 32), Cheese Biscuits, Fruited Chicken Salad (page 32), Mint Tea

 Winter
Garden Salad
Sampler

Asparagus Soup

Ham-Blue Cheese Pasta Salad

Spinach-Apple Salad
With Orange Dressing

Marinated Vegetable Medley

Poppy Seed Croissants

Butter Curls

*Chateau Biltmore Chardonnay Barrel
Fermented*

Amaretto Chantilly

Serves 8

Asparagus Soup

3 pounds fresh asparagus
2 cups water
½ cup chopped onion
2½ cups milk, divided
¼ cup butter or margarine
¼ cup all-purpose flour
2 cups half-and-half
1 teaspoon salt
¼ teaspoon ground white pepper

Snap off tough ends of asparagus. Remove scales from stalks with a vegetable peeler or knife, if desired. Cut asparagus into 1-inch pieces. Place asparagus, water, and onion in a large saucepan. Bring to a boil; cover, reduce heat, and simmer 10 to 12 minutes or until tender. Drain. Combine asparagus mixture and ½ cup milk in container of an electric blender; cover and process until smooth, stopping several times to scrape down sides. Set aside.

Melt butter in saucepan; add flour, stirring until smooth. Cook 1 minute, stirring constantly. Gradually add remaining 2 cups milk and half-and-half. Cook over medium heat, stirring constantly, until mixture is thickened and bubbly. Stir in asparagus puree, salt, and pepper. Cook until thoroughly heated. Serve warm or chilled. Yield: 2 quarts.

Ham-Blue Cheese Pasta Salad

4 cups uncooked bow tie pasta
6 ounces cooked ham, cut into strips
1 cup coarsely chopped pecans
5 ounces blue cheese, crumbled
⅓ cup chopped fresh parsley
2 tablespoons minced fresh rosemary or 2 teaspoons dried whole rosemary
½ to 1 teaspoon coarsely ground pepper
1 large clove garlic, minced
⅓ cup olive oil
⅓ cup grated Parmesan cheese

Cook pasta according to package directions; drain. Rinse with cold water, and drain.

Combine pasta and next 8 ingredients, tossing well. Sprinkle with Parmesan cheese. Serve immediately or chill, if desired. Yield: 8 servings.

Spinach-Apple Salad with Orange Dressing (page 40),
Marinated Vegetable Medley (page 40), Ham-Blue Cheese
Pasta Salad, Poppy Seed Croissants (page 40)

Spinach-Apple Salad with Orange Dressing

- 1   pound fresh spinach, stems removed
- ⅔   cup mayonnaise
- ¼   cup plus 2 tablespoons frozen orange juice concentrate, thawed
- 2   red apples, unpeeled and chopped
- 8   slices bacon, cooked and crumbled

Wash leaves, and pat dry. Tear into bite-size pieces. Combine mayonnaise and orange juice concentrate; stir well. Combine spinach, apple, and bacon. Serve with dressing. Yield: 8 servings.

Marinated Vegetable Medley

- ⅔   cup vinegar
- ⅔   cup vegetable oil
- ⅓   cup chopped onion
- 1   teaspoon sugar
- 1   teaspoon salt
- 1   teaspoon dried basil
- 1   teaspoon dried oregano
- ⅛   teaspoon garlic powder
- 1   (14-ounce) can artichoke hearts, drained and quartered
- 1   cup broccoli flowerets
- 1   cup cauliflower flowerets
- 1   cup sliced carrot
- 1   cup sliced fresh mushrooms

Combine first 8 ingredients in a small saucepan. Bring mixture to a boil; cover, reduce heat, and simmer 12 minutes. Combine vegetables and vinegar mixture, tossing gently. Cover and chill at least 3 hours. Serve with a slotted spoon. Yield: 8 servings.

Poppy Seed Croissants

- 1   cup butter, softened
- ⅔   cup plus 1 tablespoon milk, divided
- 2   packages active dry yeast
- ½   cup warm water (105° to 115°)
- 4 to 4½   cups all-purpose flour, divided
- 2   large eggs
- ¼   cup vegetable oil
- 3   tablespoons sugar
- 2   teaspoons salt
- 1   egg yolk, lightly beaten
- 1½   teaspoons poppy seeds

Strawberries 'n' Lemon Cream

½ cup whipping cream
3 tablespoons powdered sugar
½ cup sour cream
2 tablespoons lemon juice
   Garnish: fresh mint leaves
2 pints fresh strawberries

Beat whipping cream until foamy; gradually add powdered sugar, beating until soft peaks form. Combine sour cream and lemon juice; fold into whipped cream. Garnish, if desired. Serve with strawberries. Yield: 1¼ cups.

Almond Tea Tarts

1 large egg
2 tablespoons plus 2 teaspoons sugar
½ teaspoon grated orange rind
2 tablespoons plus 2 teaspoons orange juice
⅛ teaspoon almond extract
   Tea Tart Shells
3 tablespoons sliced almonds, lightly toasted
3 tablespoons apricot preserves

Beat egg until thick and pale. Add sugar, orange rind, orange juice, and almond extract; beat well. Spoon mixture into prepared Tea Tart Shells. Bake at 350° for 15 minutes or until tops are firm. Let cool in tart pans 5 minutes. Remove from pans.

Arrange almonds in a ring, flower fashion, on top of filling. Melt apricot preserves in a small saucepan over low heat, stirring often. Pour preserves through a wire-mesh strainer into a bowl, discarding apricot pulp. Spoon warm preserves evenly over almonds. Yield: 1½ dozen.

Tea Tart Shells
⅔ cup all-purpose flour
¼ teaspoon salt
¼ cup shortening
1½ to 2 tablespoons cold water

Combine flour and salt; cut in shortening with pastry blender until mixture is crumbly. Sprinkle cold water (1 tablespoon at a time) evenly over surface; stir with a fork until dry ingredients are moistened. Shape into a ball; chill 30 minutes.

Divide dough into 18 balls. Place in ungreased miniature (1¾-inch) muffin pans, shaping each into a shell. Bake at 375° for 8 to 10 minutes or until lightly browned. Let cool 5 minutes. Yield: 1½ dozen.

Dinner in the Family Dining Room

Cream of Peanut Soup

———

Beef Tenderloin
With Cognac Mustard Sauce

Potatoes Duchesse

French Beans with Garlic

Chateau Biltmore Cabernet-Sauvignon

———

Fudge Chocolate-Pecan Pie

Strawberry English Trifle

Coffee

Serves 8

Cream of Peanut Soup

1½   cups chopped onion
1   cup chopped celery
½   cup butter or margarine, melted
¼   cup all-purpose flour
4   cups chicken broth
2   cups milk
2   cups half-and-half
2   cups creamy peanut butter
¼   teaspoon salt (optional)
¼   teaspoon ground white pepper
¼   teaspoon paprika

Cook onion and celery in butter in a Dutch oven over medium-high heat, stirring constantly, 3 minutes or until tender. Add flour, stirring until smooth. Cook 1 minute, stirring constantly. Gradually add chicken broth; bring to a boil. Gradually stir in milk and half-and-half.

Remove from heat; pour mixture through a wire-mesh strainer into a large saucepan, discarding vegetables. Add peanut butter, and stir well with a wire whisk. Cook over medium heat 5 minutes or until slightly thickened and bubbly, stirring occasionally. Stir in salt, if desired, pepper, and paprika. Yield: 2½ quarts.

Beef Tenderloin with Cognac Mustard Sauce

½   cup Dijon mustard
¼   cup mayonnaise
¼   cup sour cream
2   tablespoons Cognac
1   (4-pound) beef tenderloin, trimmed
2   teaspoons freshly ground pepper

Combine first 4 ingredients in a small bowl; stir well. Cover and chill thoroughly.

Rub tenderloin with pepper, and place on a rack in a roasting pan. Insert meat thermometer into thickest portion of tenderloin. Bake, uncovered, at 425° for 30 to 45 minutes or until meat thermometer registers 145°(medium-rare) or 160°(medium). Let stand 10 minutes before slicing. Serve with mustard sauce. Yield: 8 servings.

Beef Tenderloin with Cognac Mustard Sauce, Potatoes Duchesse (page 50), French Beans with Garlic (page 50)

Potatoes Duchesse

6   cups mashed, unseasoned potato
4   egg yolks
½   cup whipping cream
1   teaspoon salt
½   teaspoon ground white pepper
½   teaspoon curry powder
2   large eggs, lightly beaten
2   tablespoons olive oil
½   teaspoon salt
½   cup sliced almonds, lightly toasted (optional)

Combine first 6 ingredients in a large mixing bowl; beat at low speed of an electric mixer until smooth. (Mixture will be stiff.)

Combine eggs, oil, and ½ teaspoon salt; beat well.

Lightly grease a large baking sheet. Spoon potato mixture into a decorating bag fitted with a large metal star tip; pipe into 16 to 20 (4½-inch) spiral shapes. Brush lightly with egg mixture, using a small, soft-bristled brush (a small art brush will help prevent disturbing the piped edges); arrange almonds on potato spirals, if desired. Bake at 400° for 25 to 30 minutes or until edges are lightly browned. Carefully transfer to a serving platter. Yield: 8 to 10 servings.

French Beans with Garlic

2   pounds fresh green beans, trimmed and cut into very thin strips
1   cup water
½   cup sliced green onions
4   cloves garlic, crushed
¼   cup plus 2 tablespoons butter or margarine, melted
¼   teaspoon salt
¼   teaspoon pepper
½   cup chopped fresh parsley
3   tablespoons lemon juice

Place green beans and water in a large Dutch oven. Bring to a boil; cover, reduce heat, and simmer 6 to 8 minutes or until crisp-tender. Drain and set aside.

Cook green onions and garlic in butter in a Dutch oven over medium heat, stirring constantly, until tender. Return beans to pan. Add salt and pepper, stirring well. Cook over medium heat 3 minutes or until thoroughly heated, stirring occasionally. Stir in parsley and lemon juice. Yield: 8 to 10 servings.

Fudge Chocolate-Pecan Pie

1	(4-ounce) package sweet baking chocolate
½	cup butter
1	(14-ounce) can sweetened condensed milk
1	cup flaked coconut
½	cup chopped pecans
½	cup hot water
1	teaspoon vanilla extract
⅛	teaspoon salt
2	large eggs, lightly beaten
1	(9-inch) unbaked pastry shell

Combine chocolate and butter in a small saucepan; cook over low heat, stirring constantly, until chocolate and butter melt. Remove from heat, and stir in condensed milk.

Combine coconut and next 5 ingredients; stir into chocolate mixture. Pour into pastry shell. Bake at 350° for 45 minutes. Yield: one 9-inch pie.

Strawberry English Trifle

⅓	cup sugar
2	teaspoons cornstarch
3	cups milk
6	large eggs, lightly beaten
2	teaspoons vanilla extract
½ to 1	cup seedless strawberry jam
24	ladyfingers, split lengthwise
¼	cup cream sherry
1	(16-ounce) can sliced peaches in heavy syrup, drained
3	bananas, sliced
1	cup whipping cream, whipped
	Garnishes: fresh strawberries, sliced almonds

Combine sugar and cornstarch in a medium saucepan; stir well. Gradually add milk; cook over medium heat, stirring constantly, until mixture thickens and comes to a boil. Boil 1 minute, stirring constantly. Remove from heat. Gradually stir about one-fourth of hot milk mixture into beaten eggs; add to remaining hot milk mixture, stirring constantly. Cook over medium heat, stirring constantly, until mixture thickens (do not boil). Remove from heat; stir in vanilla. Cool.

Spread jam between halves of ladyfingers; reassemble. Brush both sides of ladyfingers with sherry. Arrange ladyfingers in bottom of a 3-quart trifle bowl. Cover with sliced peaches and banana slices. Pour cooled custard over fruit. Cover and chill at least 2 hours. Top trifle with whipped cream. Garnish, if desired. Yield: 12 servings.

Appetizer Buffet in the Tapestry Gallery

Pesto Dip

Shrimp Pâté

Roasted Pepper Strips and Endive

Marinated Cheese

Prosciutto-Wrapped Asparagus

Biltmore Estate Sauvignon Blanc
or
Biltmore Estate Cardinal's Crest

Chocolate Truffles

Orange Dessert Cheese Mold

Biltmore Estate Blanc de Blanc Sec

Serves 25

Pesto Dip

1½ cups lightly packed fresh basil leaves
⅔   cup grated Parmesan cheese
½   cup pine nuts or chopped walnuts, toasted
¼   cup plus 2 tablespoons olive oil
2   small cloves garlic, minced
½   teaspoon salt
½   teaspoon pepper
2   (8-ounce) cartons sour cream

Combine first 7 ingredients in container of an electric blender. Cover and process at medium speed until smooth, stopping once to scrape down sides. Spoon mixture into a bowl. Stir in sour cream. Serve with fresh vegetables. Yield: 3 cups.

Shrimp Pâté

3   cups water
1   pound unpeeled medium-size fresh shrimp
½   cup butter, softened
1   (3-ounce) package cream cheese, softened
1   teaspoon chopped fresh dillweed
¼   teaspoon salt
⅛   teaspoon pepper
⅛   teaspoon chopped garlic
⅓   cup whipping cream, whipped

Bring 3 cups water to a boil; add shrimp, and cook 3 to 5 minutes. Drain; rinse with cold water. Peel and devein shrimp. Position knife blade in food processor bowl; add shrimp. Cover and process until finely chopped. Add butter and next 5 ingredients; process until smooth. Transfer mixture to mixing bowl, and fold in whipped cream.
Line a 2½-cup mold or bowl with plastic wrap, allowing edges to hang over 6 to 7 inches. Spoon shrimp mixture into mold. Fold plastic wrap over shrimp mixture. Chill at least 4 hours or until firm. Invert pâté onto a serving platter, and peel off plastic wrap. Serve pâté with assorted crackers or party breads. Yield: 2½ cups.

Roasted Pepper Strips and Endive

1   large sweet red pepper
¼   cup olive oil
1½ tablespoons balsamic vinegar
1½ tablespoons minced fresh parsley
¼   teaspoon salt
1   clove garlic, minced
    Pinch of ground white pepper
6   heads Belgian endive

Wash and dry red pepper; place on a foil-lined baking sheet. Bake at 500° for 20 to 25 minutes or until blistered. Place in a heavy-duty zip-top plastic bag; seal and let stand 10 minutes to loosen skin. Peel pepper; split pepper, if necessary, and remove and discard membranes and seeds. Cut pepper into 2- x ¼-inch strips. Set aside.

Combine oil and next 5 ingredients; add pepper strips. Cover and chill 8 hours. Rinse endive lightly; pat dry, and trim ends. Arrange on serving platter. Place a pepper strip on each endive leaf. Cover with a damp towel; chill until ready to serve. Yield: about 30 appetizers.

Marinated Cheese

        1   (0.7-ounce) envelope Italian salad dressing mix
        ½   cup vegetable oil
        ¼   cup white vinegar
        2   tablespoons water
        2   tablespoons minced green onions
      1½   teaspoons sugar
        1   (8-ounce) package Monterey Jack cheese
        1   (8-ounce) package sharp Cheddar cheese
        1   (8-ounce) package cream cheese
        1   (4-ounce) jar diced pimiento, drained
            Garnish: fresh parsley sprigs

Combine first 6 ingredients in a small jar; cover tightly, and shake vigorously. Set aside.

Cut Monterey Jack cheese crosswise into ¼-inch strips. Cut each strip in half to form 2 squares. Set aside. Repeat procedure with Cheddar cheese and cream cheese.

Arrange cheese slices alternately in a shallow baking dish, standing slices on edge. Pour dressing mixture over cheese. Cover and chill at least 8 hours. Transfer cheese slices to a serving platter in the same alternating fashion, reserving marinade. Spoon marinade over cheese slices. Top with diced pimiento. Garnish, if desired. Serve with crackers. Yield: 25 appetizer servings.

Prosciutto-Wrapped Asparagus

        50   fresh asparagus spears (about 3 pounds)
             About 2 tablespoons Dijon mustard
        50   thin slices prosciutto or fully cooked ham (about 1 pound)

Snap off tough ends of asparagus. Remove scales with a vegetable peeler or knife, if desired. Cook asparagus in a small amount of boiling water 3 to 4 minutes. Drain; plunge asparagus in ice water. Drain.

Spread about ⅛ teaspoon mustard on one side of each slice of prosciutto. Wrap prosciutto, mustard side in, around asparagus. Cover tightly, and chill up to 2 days. Yield: 25 appetizer servings.

Appetizers & Beverages

Buttery Brown Sugar Dip with Fresh Fruit

1¾ cups firmly packed brown sugar
1 cup butter
1 cup whipping cream
1 cup chopped pecans, toasted
1 tablespoon chopped pecans, toasted (optional)
3 pounds pears, cored and sliced
3 pounds apples, cored and sliced
2 pounds seedless green grapes

Combine first 4 ingredients in a heavy saucepan; cook over medium heat until butter melts, stirring occasionally. Reduce heat, and simmer 15 minutes, stirring occasionally. Transfer to a serving dish, and, if desired, sprinkle with 1 tablespoon pecans. Serve warm with fruit. Yield: 25 appetizer servings.

Crudité Dip

1 (8-ounce) carton sour cream
1 cup mayonnaise
½ cup chopped fresh parsley
3 tablespoons minced fresh chives
1 teaspoon lemon juice
¼ teaspoon salt
1 clove garlic, minced
1 large cabbage

Combine first 7 ingredients in a bowl, stirring well. Cover and chill thoroughly.
Trim core end of cabbage to form a flat base. Fold back several outer leaves of cabbage. Cut a crosswise slice from the top, removing about one-fourth of the head. Lift enough inner leaves from the cabbage to form a 1-inch-thick shell. (Reserve slice and cabbage leaves for another use.) Spoon dip into cavity of cabbage. Serve with fresh vegetables. Yield: 2 cups.

Parmesan-Cream Cheese Ball

2 (8-ounce) packages cream cheese, softened
½ cup mayonnaise or salad dressing
⅓ cup grated Parmesan cheese
10 slices bacon, cooked and crumbled
¼ cup sliced green onions

Combine first 3 ingredients in a large mixing bowl; beat at medium speed of an electric mixer until blended. Stir in bacon and green onions; cover and chill at least 3 hours. Shape mixture into a ball. Serve with assorted crackers. Yield: one (4½-inch) cheese ball.

Terrine of Duck Livers

1   medium onion, finely chopped
1   clove garlic, minced
2   tablespoons butter or margarine, melted
1   pound ground pork
1   pound ground veal
½   pound duck livers, ground*
2   ounces truffles, peeled and diced*
⅔   cup Madeira wine
1   large egg, lightly beaten
2   teaspoons salt
½   teaspoon dried thyme
¼   teaspoon ground allspice
¼   teaspoon freshly ground pepper
1   pound bacon
    Lettuce leaves
    Garnish: sweet red pepper rings

Cook onion and garlic in butter in a skillet over medium-high heat, stirring constantly, until tender. Transfer mixture to a large bowl; add ground pork and next 9 ingredients, mixing well.

Line bottom and sides of a 9- x 5- x 3-inch loafpan with two-thirds of bacon (about 12 slices). Press pork mixture into pan, and cover with remaining bacon slices. Cover tightly with aluminum foil; place loafpan in a 13- x 9- x 2-inch pan. Add hot water to larger pan to depth of 1 inch. Bake at 350° for 2 hours or until a wooden pick inserted in center comes out clean.

Remove from oven, and cool, draining off pan drippings as terrine cools. Cover with aluminum foil; place a slightly smaller pan on top of terrine, and fill with pie weights, dried beans, or unopened cans. (Weighting will compact the terrine for the shape and texture characteristic of this dish.) Chill at least 8 hours.

Discard foil wrap. Run a knife around pan to loosen bacon from sides, if necessary. Remove any gelatin that has formed; invert terrine onto a lettuce-lined platter. Garnish, if desired. Serve with melba rounds. Yield: 18 to 20 servings.

*Chicken livers may be substituted for duck livers. Woodland mushrooms may be substituted for truffles.

Hot Artichoke-Crabmeat Spread

2 (9-ounce) packages frozen artichoke hearts
8 ounces fresh crabmeat, drained and flaked
1 cup grated Parmesan cheese
1 cup mayonnaise
¼ teaspoon lemon-pepper seasoning
2 cloves garlic, minced

Cook artichokes according to package directions; drain well, and chop. Add crabmeat and remaining ingredients; stir well. Spoon into a greased 10- x 6- x 2-inch baking dish; bake, uncovered, at 350° for 20 minutes or until hot. Serve with assorted crackers. Yield: about 3½ cups.

Cucumber Canapés

3 (3-ounce) packages cream cheese, softened
2 tablespoons mayonnaise
1½ tablespoons minced fresh parsley
1 tablespoon minced fresh dillweed
¼ teaspoon paprika
20 slices whole wheat bread
2 medium cucumbers, scored and sliced
Garnishes: radish slices, fresh dillweed sprigs

Combine first 5 ingredients in a bowl; stir well. Spoon mixture into a decorating bag fitted with a large metal star tip. Cut bread slices into 40 rounds with a 2-inch cutter. Place 1 cucumber slice on each round; pipe cream cheese mixture on top. Garnish, if desired. Yield: 40 appetizers.

Pimiento Cheese Party Sandwiches

2 cups (8 ounces) shredded extra-sharp Cheddar cheese
¼ cup plus 2 tablespoons chopped pecans
¼ cup plus 2 tablespoons mayonnaise
1 (2-ounce) jar diced pimiento, drained
6 pimiento-stuffed olives, diced
1 tablespoon dry sherry
¼ teaspoon hot sauce
⅛ to ¼ teaspoon pepper
3 (24-ounce) loaves sandwich bread
Garnish: pimiento-stuffed olive slices

Combine first 8 ingredients; stir well. Cover and chill thoroughly. Cut bread slices with a 2-inch daisy-shaped cutter. Spread cheese mixture evenly on half of bread rounds; top with remaining rounds. Garnish, if desired. Yield: 4 dozen.

Eggs à l'Italienne

6 large hard-cooked eggs
½ cup butter, softened
3 tablespoons milk
2 tablespoons soft breadcrumbs
1 tablespoon minced onion
1 tablespoon chopped fresh parsley
¼ teaspoon ground nutmeg
¼ teaspoon pepper
1 anchovy, mashed
Fresh parsley sprigs

Slice eggs in half lengthwise, and carefully remove yolks; set aside.

Beat butter at medium speed of an electric mixer until creamy. Add yolks, milk, and next 6 ingredients; beat until smooth. Spoon yolk mixture into a decorating bag fitted with a large metal star tip; pipe yolk mixture into egg whites. Top each stuffed egg with a sprig of parsley. Yield: 12 servings.

Phyllo Cheese Triangles

2 cups (8 ounces) shredded Muenster cheese
1 cup (4 ounces) shredded extra-sharp Cheddar cheese
¼ cup chopped fresh parsley
1 large egg, lightly beaten
Dash of ground red pepper
10 sheets frozen phyllo pastry, thawed
1 cup butter or margarine, melted

Combine first 5 ingredients; stir well, and set aside.

Cut sheets of phyllo lengthwise into 3-inch strips. Working with one strip at a time (keep remaining strips covered), brush strip lightly with melted butter. Place 2 teaspoons cheese mixture at base of phyllo strip; fold the right bottom corner over cheese mixture to form a triangle. Continue folding back and forth into a triangle to end of strip. Place triangle, seam side down, on an ungreased baking sheet. (Keep triangles covered before baking.) Repeat procedure with remaining phyllo strips, melted butter, and cheese mixture. Brush with remaining butter. Bake at 400° for 10 minutes or until golden. Serve immediately. Yield: 40 appetizers.

Roasted Pecan Cream Soup

½	cup pecan halves
1	tablespoon butter, melted
1	cup half-and-half
1	small onion, finely chopped
¼	cup butter, melted
¼	cup all-purpose flour
4	cups chicken broth
⅛ to ¼	teaspoon salt
⅛	teaspoon pepper
¼	cup plus 2 tablespoons whipping cream
2	egg yolks, lightly beaten
	Fried Croutons

Cook pecans in butter in a saucepan until lightly browned. Position knife blade in food processor bowl; add pecans. Pulse 8 to 10 times or until pecans are coarsely chopped. Combine pecans and half-and-half in a small saucepan; bring to a boil over medium-high heat. Remove from heat, and let stand 30 minutes.

Cook onion in butter in a large Dutch oven over medium heat until tender. Add flour; cook, stirring constantly, until roux is golden (4 minutes). Gradually add chicken broth, salt, and pepper. Bring mixture to a boil; reduce heat, and simmer 7 to 10 minutes. Stir in pecan mixture.

Combine whipping cream and egg yolks, beating well. Gradually stir about one-fourth of hot mixture into yolk mixture; add to remaining hot mixture, stirring constantly. Cook 5 minutes or until thickened, stirring occasionally (do not boil). Sprinkle each serving with Fried Croutons. Yield: 5½ cups.

Fried Croutons

1 to 2	tablespoons butter or margarine, softened
3	(¾-inch-thick) slices French bread

Spread butter on both sides of each bread slice. Cut slices into ¾-inch cubes; arrange cubes on a baking sheet. Bake at 350° for 15 minutes or until golden, stirring occasionally. Cool. Yield: 1¾ cups.

Garden in a Bowl

1   medium eggplant (about 1 pound)
1   medium-size green pepper, seeded and diced
1   medium-size purple onion, diced
1   large tomato, seeded and chopped
2   tablespoons olive oil
2   tablespoons lemon juice
1   tablespoon balsamic vinegar
1   teaspoon freshly ground pepper
1   (1-pound) round loaf Hawaiian bread

Place eggplant on a greased baking sheet; prick several times with a fork. Bake at 400° for 20 to 25 minutes or until tender. Let cool completely. Peel, seed, and chop eggplant; place in a large bowl. Add green pepper and next 6 ingredients; toss well. Cover and chill at least 2 hours.

Cut top from loaf; scoop out center, leaving a ½-inch shell. (Reserve remaining bread for another use.) Fill shell with eggplant mixture. Serve with assorted party breads. Yield: 4¼ cups.

Pineapple Punch

2   cups water
3½   cups sugar, divided
1   medium-size fresh pineapple, peeled, cored, and cubed
¼   cup lemon juice
1¼   cups brandy
1   (25.4-ounce) bottle dry champagne
¼   teaspoon cream of tartar
⅓   cup hot water
3   egg whites

Combine 2 cups water and 2½ cups sugar in a large saucepan. Bring to a boil; cook, stirring constantly, until sugar dissolves. Let cool; cover and chill. Position knife blade in food processor bowl; add pineapple, and process until pureed. Combine sugar syrup, pineapple puree, lemon juice, brandy, and champagne in an airtight container. Cover and freeze at least 8 hours.

Combine remaining 1 cup sugar, cream of tartar, and hot water in a heavy saucepan. Cook over medium heat, stirring constantly, until sugar dissolves. Cook, without stirring, until candy thermometer registers 240° (about 8 minutes). Beat egg whites at high speed of an electric mixer until stiff peaks form. Gradually pour sugar mixture in a thin stream over beaten egg whites while beating constantly at high speed. Continue to beat until egg white mixture is cool and set. Cover and chill until ready to serve.

Let pineapple mixture stand at room temperature 1 hour before serving. Place in a large punch bowl; break up mixture with a large metal spoon until slushy. Fold in egg white mixture, and serve immediately. Yield: 3 quarts.

Buttery Brown Sugar Dip with Fresh Fruit (page 62), Pineapple Punch

Syllabub

1 cup dry white wine
¼ cup brandy
¼ cup sugar
1 tablespoon lemon juice
2 cups whipping cream, whipped

Combine first 4 ingredients, stirring until sugar dissolves. Add whipped cream, stirring well. Spoon mixture into stemmed goblets, and serve immediately. Yield: 5½ cups.

Lemonade

3 lemons
1 cup sugar
5 cups water, divided
1 cup fresh lemon juice

Peel lemons, leaving pith on fruit. Cut lemon rind into ¼-inch strips. Combine lemon strips, sugar, and 2 cups water in a medium saucepan. Bring to a boil; boil 7 minutes. Let cool.

Transfer mixture to a pitcher, discarding lemon strips, if desired. Add remaining 3 cups water and lemon juice; stir well. Cover and chill thoroughly. Yield: 1½ quarts.

Spiced Cranberry Tea

1½ teaspoons whole allspice
1 teaspoon whole cloves
2 (3-inch) sticks cinnamon
3 cups boiling water
2 regular-size tea bags
1 cup cranberry juice cocktail
2 to 4 tablespoons honey
Garnish: orange slices

Place first 3 ingredients on a piece of cheesecloth; tie ends of cheesecloth securely.

Pour boiling water over cheesecloth bag and tea bags in a teapot or saucepan; cover and steep 5 minutes. Remove and discard cheesecloth bag and tea bags, squeezing gently. Stir in cranberry juice and honey. Serve over ice; garnish, if desired. Yield: 1 quart.

Breads

Soda Biscuits

    2   cups all-purpose flour
    2   teaspoons baking powder
    ¾   teaspoon salt
    ⅓   cup shortening
    ¾   cup plus 1 tablespoon buttermilk
    ½   teaspoon baking soda

Combine first 3 ingredients in a medium bowl; cut in shortening with a pastry blender until mixture is crumbly. Combine buttermilk and soda; stir well. Add to flour mixture, stirring just until dry ingredients are moistened.

Turn dough out onto a lightly floured surface, and knead 5 or 6 times. Roll dough to ½-inch thickness; cut into rounds with a 2-inch biscuit cutter. Place rounds on a lightly greased baking sheet. Bake at 450° for 10 minutes or until biscuits are golden. Yield: 16 biscuits.

Currant Scones

    1   cup all-purpose flour
    1   teaspoon baking powder
    ⅛   teaspoon baking soda
    1½   tablespoons sugar
    ¼   teaspoon grated orange rind
    ¼   cup butter or margarine
    ¼   cup currants
    ¼   cup buttermilk
    ½   teaspoon sugar
    ⅛   teaspoon ground cinnamon

Combine first 5 ingredients in a medium bowl; cut in butter with a pastry blender until mixture is crumbly. Add currants, tossing lightly. Add buttermilk, stirring until dry ingredients are moistened.

Turn dough out onto a lightly floured surface, and knead 5 or 6 times; shape into a ball. Place in a greased 8-inch round cakepan, and flatten to a 7-inch circle. Combine ½ teaspoon sugar and cinnamon; sprinkle over top. Bake at 375° for 10 minutes. Remove from oven; cut an **X** about ½ inch deep across top. Bake an additional 20 minutes or until golden. Serve warm. Yield: 4 to 6 servings.

Griddle Cakes

  2 cups all-purpose flour
  1 teaspoon baking soda
  ½ teaspoon salt
  1 tablespoon sugar
  2 large eggs, separated
2½ cups buttermilk

Combine first 4 ingredients in a large bowl; stir well. Make a well in center of mixture.

Beat egg yolks until thick and pale; stir in buttermilk. Add to dry ingredients, stirring just until moistened.

Beat egg whites at high speed of an electric mixer until soft peaks form. Gently fold egg white into flour mixture.

For each pancake, pour about ¼ cup batter onto a hot, lightly greased griddle; spread to a 4-inch circle. Cook pancakes until tops are covered with bubbles and edges look cooked; turn and cook other side. Serve with fresh strawberries and hot syrup. Yield: 20 pancakes.

Old-Fashioned Blueberry Muffins

  2 cups all-purpose flour
  1 tablespoon baking powder
  ½ teaspoon salt
  ⅔ cup sugar
  ½ teaspoon ground nutmeg
  2 large eggs, lightly beaten
  ½ cup milk
  ½ cup butter or margarine, melted
1½ cups fresh blueberries
  ¼ cup sliced almonds
  1 tablespoon sugar

Combine first 5 ingredients in a large bowl, setting aside 1 tablespoon of mixture to toss with blueberries. Make a well in center of mixture.

Combine eggs, milk, and butter; add to dry ingredients, stirring just until moistened. Toss blueberries with 1 tablespoon flour mixture; fold into batter. Spoon batter into greased muffin pans, filling two-thirds full. Sprinkle evenly with almonds and 1 tablespoon sugar. Bake at 400° for 15 to 18 minutes. Remove from pans immediately. Yield: 1½ dozen.

Lemon-Raspberry Muffins

2   cups all-purpose flour
1   tablespoon baking powder
½   teaspoon salt
¾   cup sugar
1   cup fresh raspberries
2   large eggs, lightly beaten
1   cup half-and-half
½   cup vegetable oil
1   teaspoon lemon extract
    Vegetable cooking spray

Combine first 5 ingredients in a large bowl; make a well in center of mixture. Combine eggs and next 3 ingredients; add to dry ingredients, stirring just until moistened.

Place paper baking cups in muffin pans; coat with cooking spray. Spoon batter into cups, filling three-fourths full. Bake at 425° for 20 to 22 minutes. Remove from pans immediately. Yield: 1½ dozen.

Carrot-Pineapple Bread

1   (8-ounce) can crushed pineapple, undrained
¾   cup firmly packed brown sugar
3   tablespoons vegetable oil
1   large egg, lightly beaten
2   teaspoons grated orange rind
1½   cups all-purpose flour
1   cup whole wheat flour
1   tablespoon plus ½ teaspoon baking powder
½   teaspoon ground nutmeg
1   cup chopped pecans
1   cup shredded carrot

Drain pineapple, reserving juice; set pineapple aside. Add enough water to pineapple juice to measure ¾ cup.

Combine brown sugar, oil, and egg in a large bowl; stir well. Add pineapple, juice mixture, and orange rind; stir well. Combine flours, baking powder, and nutmeg; add to pineapple mixture, stirring just until blended. Stir in pecans and carrot.

Pour batter into a greased 9- x 5- x 3-inch loafpan. Bake at 350° for 1 hour to 1 hour and 10 minutes or until a wooden pick inserted in center comes out clean. Cool in pan on a wire rack 10 minutes. Remove from pan, and let cool completely on a wire rack. Yield: 1 loaf.

Cranberry-Orange Nut Bread

2	cups all-purpose flour
1½	teaspoons baking powder
½	teaspoon salt
1	cup sugar
½	cup boiling water
1½	teaspoons grated orange rind
¼	cup orange juice
2	tablespoons shortening, melted
1	large egg, lightly beaten
1	cup chopped walnuts
1	cup fresh cranberries, coarsely chopped

Combine first 4 ingredients in a large bowl; make a well in center of mixture. Combine water and next 4 ingredients; stir well. Add to dry ingredients, stirring just until moistened. Stir in walnuts and cranberries.

Pour batter into a greased 8½- x 4½- x 3-inch loafpan. Bake at 350° for 1 hour and 15 minutes or until a wooden pick inserted in center comes out clean. Cool in pan on a wire rack 10 minutes. Remove from pan, and let cool completely on a wire rack. Yield: 1 loaf.

Walnut-Banana Bread

3¼	cups all-purpose flour
2	teaspoons baking soda
1	teaspoon salt
1⅔	cups sugar
1	cup butter, melted
2	large bananas, peeled and mashed
2	large eggs, lightly beaten
2	tablespoons water
1¼	cups chopped walnuts

Combine first 4 ingredients in a large bowl; make a well in center of mixture. Combine butter and next 3 ingredients, stirring well; add to dry ingredients, stirring just until moistened. Stir in walnuts.

Pour batter into 2 greased and floured 8½- x 4½- x 3-inch loafpans. Bake at 350° for 45 minutes or until a wooden pick inserted in center comes out clean. Cool in pans on wire racks 10 minutes. Remove from pans, and let cool completely on wire racks. Yield: 2 loaves.

Apple-Date Nut Ring

       2 packages active dry yeast
       ½ cup warm water (105° to 115°)
       ¾ cup milk
       ½ cup sugar
       ½ cup butter or margarine
       ½ teaspoon salt
       1 large egg, lightly beaten
4 to 4¾ cups all-purpose flour, divided
       2 tablespoons butter or margarine, melted
       2 cups peeled, finely chopped apple
       1 (8-ounce) package pitted dates, chopped
       ½ cup chopped walnuts
       ¼ cup sugar
       2 teaspoons ground cinnamon
       2 cups sifted powdered sugar
       3 tablespoons milk
       ¼ teaspoon vanilla extract

Combine yeast and warm water in a 1-cup liquid measuring cup; let stand 5 minutes. Combine ¾ cup milk and next 3 ingredients in a saucepan; heat until butter melts, stirring occasionally. Cool to 105° to 115°.

Combine yeast mixture, milk mixture, egg, and 2 cups flour in a large mixing bowl; beat at low speed of an electric mixer just until blended. Stir in enough of remaining flour to make a soft dough. Turn dough out onto a floured surface, and knead until smooth and elastic (about 5 minutes). Place in a well-greased bowl, turning to grease top. Cover and refrigerate 8 hours.

Punch dough down, and divide in half; roll each portion into a 14- x 9-inch rectangle, and brush each with 1 tablespoon butter. Combine apple and next 4 ingredients; spoon half of mixture evenly over each rectangle of dough to within ½ inch of edges.

Roll up each rectangle, jellyroll fashion, starting with long side; moisten edges with water, and pinch to seal. Place each on a greased 12-inch pizza pan, seam side down; shape each into a ring. Pinch ends together to seal.

Using kitchen shears, make cuts in dough at 1-inch intervals around rings, cutting two-thirds of the way through rolls. Gently turn each piece of dough on its side, slightly overlapping slices. Cover and let rise in a warm place (85°), free from drafts, 45 minutes or until doubled in bulk. Bake at 350° for 20 to 25 minutes or until golden. Cool slightly. Combine powdered sugar, 3 tablespoons milk, and vanilla; stir until smooth. Drizzle half over each ring. Yield: 2 rings.

Apple-Date Nut Ring, Old-Fashioned Cinnamon Rolls (page 78)

Old-Fashioned Cinnamon Rolls

1	package active dry yeast
½	cup warm water (105° to 115°)
½	cup boiling water
¼	cup shortening
¼	cup butter or margarine
¾	cup sugar, divided
1	large egg
1	egg yolk
1½	teaspoons salt
3¾ to 4	cups bread flour, divided
¼	cup butter or margarine, softened
⅔	cup chopped pecans
½	cup raisins
2	teaspoons ground cinnamon
1½	cups sifted powdered sugar
2	tablespoons milk
½	teaspoon vanilla extract

Combine yeast and ½ cup warm water; let stand 5 minutes. Combine boiling water, shortening, butter, and ½ cup sugar in a mixing bowl; stir until shortening melts. Cool to 105° to 115°. Add yeast mixture, egg, egg yolk, and salt; beat well at medium speed of an electric mixer. Add 2 cups flour; beat at medium speed until smooth. Stir in enough of remaining flour to make a soft dough.

Turn dough out onto a lightly floured surface, and knead until smooth and elastic (about 5 to 7 minutes). Place in a well-greased bowl, turning to grease top. Cover and let rise in a warm place (85°), free from drafts, 1½ hours or until doubled in bulk.

Punch dough down; divide in half. Roll each half into a 15- x 9-inch rectangle. Spread rectangles with butter; sprinkle with pecans and raisins. Combine remaining ¼ cup sugar and cinnamon; sprinkle over rectangles. Roll up each rectangle, jellyroll fashion, starting with long side. Cut each roll into 9 slices; place slices, cut side down, in two greased 9-inch square pans. Cover and let rise 1 hour or until doubled in bulk. Bake at 350° for 20 to 25 minutes or until golden. Combine powdered sugar, milk, and vanilla; drizzle evenly over warm rolls. Yield: 1½ dozen.

Sour Cream Yeast Rolls

½	cup sour cream
¼	cup butter or margarine
¼	cup sugar
½	teaspoon salt
1	package active dry yeast
¼	cup warm water (105° to 115°)
1	large egg, lightly beaten
2½	cups all-purpose flour, divided
1	egg white, lightly beaten

Combine first 4 ingredients in a small saucepan; cook over medium heat until butter melts, stirring occasionally. Cool to 105° to 115°.

Combine yeast and warm water in a 1-cup liquid measuring cup; let stand 5 minutes. Combine sour cream mixture, yeast mixture, egg, and 1½ cups flour in a large mixing bowl; beat at medium speed of an electric mixer 2 minutes. Gradually stir in remaining 1 cup flour to make a soft dough (dough will be sticky). Cover and refrigerate 8 hours.

Punch dough down; divide in half. Roll each portion into a 12-inch circle on a floured surface. Cut each circle into 12 wedges; roll up each wedge, beginning at wide end. Place rolls, point side down, on greased baking sheets. Cover and let rise in a warm place (85°), free from drafts, 45 minutes or until doubled in bulk. Gently brush rolls with egg white. Bake at 350° for 10 minutes or until golden. Yield: 2 dozen.

Potato Rolls

½   cup peeled, diced baking potato (about ¼ pound)
2   cups milk
¼   cup butter
1   teaspoon salt
3½ to 4   cups all-purpose flour, divided
1   tablespoon sugar
1   package active dry yeast
2   tablespoons butter, melted

Cook potato in a small amount of boiling water 15 minutes or until tender; drain. Mash potato. Combine potato, milk, ¼ cup butter, and salt in a saucepan; heat until butter melts, stirring occasionally. Cool to 120° to 130°.

Combine 2 cups flour, sugar, and yeast in a mixing bowl; stir well. Gradually add liquid mixture to flour mixture, beating well at low speed of an electric mixer. Beat an additional 2 minutes at medium speed. Gradually add ¾ cup flour, beating 2 minutes at medium speed. Gradually stir in enough of remaining flour to make a soft dough.

Turn dough out onto a well-floured surface, and knead until smooth and elastic (about 10 minutes). Place in a well-greased bowl, turning to grease top. Cover and let rise in a warm place (85°), free from drafts, 1 hour or until doubled in bulk.

Punch dough down; turn out onto a lightly floured surface, and knead lightly 4 or 5 times. Roll dough to 1-inch thickness; cut into rounds with a 3-inch cutter. Place rounds on a lightly greased baking sheet; brush lightly with melted butter. Fold rounds in half; brush tops with remaining melted butter. Cover and let rise in a warm place, free from drafts, 20 minutes or until doubled in bulk. Bake at 400° for 12 to 15 minutes or until golden. Yield: 27 rolls.

Butterflake Herb Loaf

½ cup butter or margarine, softened
½ teaspoon caraway seeds
½ teaspoon dried basil
½ teaspoon grated onion
¼ teaspoon dried oregano
¼ teaspoon garlic powder
⅛ teaspoon ground red pepper
5 to 5½ cups all-purpose flour, divided
¼ cup sugar
1 tablespoon salt
1 package active dry yeast
1½ cups milk
⅓ cup shortening
2 large eggs

Combine first 7 ingredients in a small bowl, stirring well; set butter mixture aside.

Combine 2 cups flour and next 3 ingredients in a large mixing bowl; stir well. Combine milk and shortening in a small saucepan; heat until shortening melts, stirring occasionally. Cool to 120° to 130°. Gradually add liquid mixture to flour mixture, beating well at low speed of an electric mixer. Beat an additional 2 minutes at medium speed. Add eggs, beating well. Gradually stir in enough of remaining flour to make a soft dough.

Turn dough out onto a lightly floured surface, and knead until smooth and elastic (about 5 minutes). Shape into a ball, and place in a well-greased bowl, turning to grease top. Cover and let rise in a warm place (85°), free from drafts, 1 hour or until doubled in bulk.

Punch dough down, and divide in half. Roll one portion into a 15- x 9-inch rectangle; spread rectangle with half of butter mixture. Roll up, jellyroll fashion, starting with short side; pinch seam and ends to seal. Place loaf, seam side down, in a well-greased 9- x 5- x 3-inch loafpan. Repeat procedure with remaining dough and butter mixture. Cover and let rise in a warm place, free from drafts, 40 minutes or until doubled in bulk. Bake at 350° for 25 to 30 minutes or until loaves sound hollow when tapped. Yield: 2 loaves.

Sesame Seed French Bread (page 82), Sour Cream Yeast
Rolls (page 78), Butterflake Herb Loaf

Sesame Seed French Bread

2 packages active dry yeast
2½ teaspoons sugar
½ cup warm water (105° to 115°)
1 cup boiling water
2 tablespoons sugar
2 tablespoons butter or margarine
2 teaspoons salt
1 cup cold water
6½ to 7 cups all-purpose flour, divided
1 large egg, lightly beaten
2 tablespoons milk
Sesame seeds

Combine first 3 ingredients in a 1-cup liquid measuring cup; let stand 5 minutes.

Combine boiling water and next 3 ingredients in a large mixing bowl; stir until butter melts. Add cold water; cool to 105° to 115°. Add yeast mixture and 2½ cups flour to water mixture; beat at medium speed of an electric mixer until blended. Gradually stir in enough of remaining flour to make a soft dough.

Turn dough out onto a lightly floured surface, and knead until smooth and elastic (about 10 minutes). Place in a well-greased bowl, turning to grease top. Cover and let rise in a warm place (85°), free from drafts, 1 hour or until doubled in bulk.

Punch dough down, and divide into 3 equal portions. Roll one portion into a 13- x 8-inch rectangle on a lightly floured surface. Roll up dough, jellyroll fashion, starting with long side, pressing firmly to eliminate air pockets; pinch seam and ends to seal. Place dough, seam side down, on a greased baking sheet. Repeat procedure with remaining portions of dough.

Cover and let rise in a warm place, free from drafts, 40 minutes or until doubled in bulk. Make diagonal slits about ¼ inch deep down top of each loaf, using a sharp knife. Combine egg and milk in a small bowl, beating well; gently brush over loaves. Sprinkle loaves with sesame seeds. Bake at 400° for 20 to 25 minutes or until loaves sound hollow when tapped. Yield: 3 loaves.

Entrées

Individual Beef Wellingtons

6	(4- to 5-ounce) beef tenderloin steaks
1	teaspoon salt
¼	teaspoon pepper
½	cup chopped onion
½	cup chopped carrot
½	cup chopped celery
2	tablespoons vegetable oil
1	cup dry red wine
2	tablespoons brandy (optional)
½	teaspoon fines herbes
1	pound fresh mushrooms, finely chopped
¼	cup minced green onions
2	tablespoons butter, melted
¾	cup Madeira wine, divided
	Salt and pepper to taste
1	tablespoon butter, melted
7	frozen puff pastry shells, thawed
1	egg yolk, lightly beaten
1	teaspoon water
2	cups beef broth
1	tablespoon tomato paste
2	tablespoons cornstarch
	Garnish: baby carrots, fresh watercress

Place steaks in a shallow dish; sprinkle with 1 teaspoon salt and ¼ teaspoon pepper. Cook onion, carrot, and celery in hot oil in a saucepan over medium-high heat, stirring constantly, until tender. Stir in dry red wine, brandy, and fines herbes. Pour over steaks. Cover and chill 8 hours.

Cook mushrooms and green onions in 2 tablespoons butter in a large skillet over medium-high heat until all liquid evaporates. Add ½ cup Madeira; cook until liquid evaporates. Stir in salt and pepper to taste. Transfer to a bowl; cover and chill thoroughly.

Drain steaks, reserving marinade. Cook steaks in 1 tablespoon butter in a nonstick skillet over medium-high heat until lightly browned on both sides.

Roll each of 6 pastry shells into a 7-inch square on a lightly floured surface; spread each square with ⅓ cup mushroom mixture, leaving ½-inch margin on all sides. Top each with a steak. Combine egg yolk and water; brush edges of pastries with egg yolk mixture. Stretch pastry over each steak, and pinch edges to seal. Place, seam side down, on rack of a broiler pan. Brush each pastry with egg yolk mixture. Roll remaining pastry shell to ⅛-inch thickness; cut into decorative shapes. Arrange shapes on tops of pastries as desired. Brush with remaining egg yolk mixture. Bake, uncovered, at 400° for 25 minutes or until golden.

Combine reserved marinade, beef broth, and tomato paste in a large saucepan. Bring to a boil; cover, reduce heat, and simmer 1 hour. Combine cornstarch and remaining ¼ cup Madeira; add to broth mixture, stirring well. Cook over medium heat, stirring constantly, until thickened. Serve with Beef Wellingtons. Garnish, if desired. Serve with *Biltmore Estate Merlot* or *Chateau Biltmore Cabernet-Sauvignon.* Yield: 6 servings.

Medaillons of Beef with Horseradish Cream

¼	cup red wine vinegar
2	tablespoons vegetable oil
¼	teaspoon salt
¼	teaspoon dried thyme
¼	teaspoon black pepper
4	(1-inch-thick) beef tenderloin steaks (about 1 pound)
½	pound carrots, scraped and cut into very thin strips
2	tablespoons butter or margarine
¼	teaspoon salt
¼	teaspoon ground nutmeg
⅛	teaspoon ground white pepper
	Horseradish Cream
	Garnish: diced carrot

Combine first 5 ingredients in a shallow dish. Add steaks, turning to coat both sides. Cover and marinate in refrigerator 4 hours, turning once.

Cook carrot strips in water to cover 4 minutes or until crisp-tender; drain. Add butter and next 3 ingredients to carrots; set aside, and keep warm.

Remove steaks from marinade, reserving marinade. Grill steaks, covered, over medium coals (300° to 350°) or broil 5½ inches from heat (with electric oven door partially opened) 3 to 4 minutes on each side or to desired degree of doneness, basting with reserved marinade mixture just before turning.

Place each steak in center of individual dinner plates. Spoon 3 tablespoons Horseradish Cream on each plate on one side of steak; place carrot strips on plate on other side. Garnish, if desired. Serve with *Biltmore Estate Sauvignon Blanc* or *Chateau Biltmore Pinot Noir.* Yield: 4 servings.

Horseradish Cream

1¼	cups whipping cream
2½	tablespoons prepared horseradish
⅛	teaspoon salt
⅛	teaspoon black pepper
	Pinch of ground nutmeg

Heat whipping cream in a heavy saucepan until reduced to about ¾ cup (do not boil). Add horseradish and remaining ingredients; cook over low heat just until mixture is thoroughly heated, stirring frequently. Yield: ¾ cup.

Spicy Rib-Eye Roast

1	(6-pound) boneless rib-eye roast
⅓ to ½	cup coarsely ground or cracked pepper
½	teaspoon ground cardamom
1	cup soy sauce
¾	cup red wine vinegar
1	tablespoon tomato paste
1	teaspoon paprika
½	teaspoon garlic powder

Trim fat from roast. Combine pepper and cardamom; rub mixture over surface of roast. Place roast in a large, shallow dish. Combine soy sauce and remaining ingredients; pour over roast. Cover and marinate in refrigerator 8 hours, turning occasionally.

Remove roast from marinade; discard marinade. Wrap roast in aluminum foil, and place in a shallow roasting pan. Insert meat thermometer into thickest part of roast, making an opening so thermometer does not touch foil. Bake at 325° for 2 hours or until meat thermometer registers 145° (medium-rare). Serve with *Biltmore Estate Cabernet-Sauvignon* or *Chateau Biltmore Merlot*. Yield: 12 to 14 servings.

Lemon Veal with Artichoke Hearts

⅓	cup all-purpose flour
¼	teaspoon salt
1	pound (¼-inch-thick) veal cutlets
2	tablespoons butter or margarine
1	cup chicken broth
¼	cup fresh lemon juice
¼	cup dry vermouth
2	tablespoons Worcestershire sauce
1	teaspoon dried marjoram
½	teaspoon minced garlic
1	bay leaf
1	(14-ounce) can artichoke hearts, drained
	Hot cooked noodles
	Garnishes: lemon slices, fresh parsley sprigs

Combine flour and salt; dredge veal in flour mixture. Melt butter in a large skillet over medium heat. Add veal, and cook 1 minute on each side; remove and drain on paper towels. Add broth and next 6 ingredients to skillet; bring to a boil, stirring frequently. Add veal and artichokes; cover, reduce heat, and simmer about 5 minutes. Remove and discard bay leaf. Serve over noodles. Garnish, if desired. Serve with *Biltmore Estate Chardonnay sur Lies* or *Biltmore Estate Cardinal's Crest*. Yield: 4 servings.

Veal Roast with Vegetables

1	(2½- to 3-pound) boneless veal sirloin roast
¼	cup plus 2 tablespoons butter or margarine, melted
½	cup chicken broth
½	cup dry white wine
½	pound medium-size fresh mushrooms
1	cup pearl onions, peeled
5	medium carrots, scraped and cut into 1-inch pieces
3	stalks celery, cut into 1-inch pieces
½	teaspoon salt
½	teaspoon pepper
	Garnish: celery leaves

Cook roast in butter in a Dutch oven over medium-high heat until browned on all sides. Add broth and wine; cover, reduce heat, and simmer 1 hour and 15 minutes. Add mushrooms and next 5 ingredients; cover and simmer 30 minutes or until vegetables and meat are tender.

Place roast on a serving platter; arrange vegetables on platter. Spoon pan juices over roast. Garnish, if desired. Serve with *Biltmore Estate "Nouveau" Red*, *Biltmore Estate Cabernet-Franc*, or *Biltmore Estate Chardonnay sur Lies*. Yield: 6 servings.

Marinated Leg of Lamb

1	(5- to 6-pound) leg of lamb, boned and butterflied
2	cups olive oil
½	cup lemon juice
1	small onion, thinly sliced
1	tablespoon minced garlic
1	tablespoon dried oregano
2	teaspoons salt
1½	teaspoons pepper
2	bay leaves

Trim fat from lamb. Place lamb in a 13- x 9- x 2-inch baking dish. Combine oil and remaining ingredients, stirring well. Pour over lamb. Cover and marinate in refrigerator 8 hours, turning occasionally.

Remove lamb from marinade; discard marinade. Grill lamb, covered, over medium coals (300° to 350°) 20 minutes; turn lamb, and insert meat thermometer into thickest part of meat. Grill 20 minutes or until meat thermometer registers 150° (medium-rare) or 160° (medium). Let stand 10 minutes. Slice diagonally across grain into thin slices. Serve with *Chateau Biltmore Vanderbilt Claret* or *Chateau Biltmore Cabernet-Sauvignon*. Yield: 8 servings.

Baked Saddle of Lamb

      2   (2-pound) racks of lamb (16 chops)
      2   tablespoons olive oil
      1   tablespoon all-purpose flour
      ½   teaspoon salt
      ½   teaspoon pepper
          Herb Gravy
          Mint Sauce

Trim exterior fat on racks to ¼ inch. Combine oil and next 3 ingredients, stirring well. Rub oil mixture over lamb. Place lamb, bone side down, on a rack in a roasting pan. Insert meat thermometer, if desired, making sure it does not touch fat or bone. Bake at 375° for 50 minutes or until meat thermometer registers 150° (medium-rare) or 160° (medium). Remove from oven, and let stand 10 minutes before slicing. Accompany with Herb Gravy and Mint Sauce. Serve with *Chateau Biltmore Merlot* or *Biltmore Estate Cardinal's Crest*. Yield: 8 servings.

Herb Gravy

    1¾   cups beef broth
      3   tablespoons minced onion
      3   tablespoons minced carrot
      1   tablespoon minced celery
      ½   teaspoon dried rosemary
      ½   teaspoon dried thyme
      2   fresh parsley sprigs
      1   bay leaf
      ½   cup dry vermouth
      1   tablespoon tomato paste
      1   tablespoon arrowroot
      1   tablespoon water

Combine first 8 ingredients in a saucepan; bring to a boil. Reduce heat, and simmer, uncovered, 20 minutes. Pour broth through a wire-mesh strainer into a bowl, discarding vegetables and bay leaf. Return broth to saucepan; stir in vermouth and tomato paste.

Combine arrowroot and water, stirring until smooth; add to broth, and stir well. Cook over medium heat, stirring constantly, until thickened and bubbly. Yield: 1½ cups.

Mint Sauce

      ¼   cup chopped fresh mint
      ¼   cup light corn syrup
    1½   tablespoons white vinegar
    1½   teaspoons cornstarch
      ¼   cup water

Combine first 3 ingredients in a small saucepan. Combine cornstarch and water; add to mint mixture. Cook over medium heat, stirring constantly, until thickened and bubbly. Yield: ½ cup.

Stuffed Crown Pork Roast

1	(12-rib) crown roast of pork, well trimmed (about 7 pounds)
½	teaspoon salt
½	teaspoon pepper
1	(6-ounce) package long-grain and wild rice mix
1	cup raisins
2	cups chicken broth
½	cup drained canned garbanzo beans or chick-peas, rinsed
½	cup chopped pecans, toasted
½	cup sliced green onions
	Garnish: kale, apple wedges, grapes, green onion ribbons

Fold a piece of aluminum foil into an 8-inch square; place on a rack in a roasting pan. Sprinkle roast with salt and pepper; place, bone ends up, on foil-lined rack. Bake at 325° for 1 hour.

Combine rice mix, seasoning pack from rice mix, raisins, and chicken broth; bring to a boil. Cover, reduce heat, and simmer 20 minutes or until rice is tender and liquid is absorbed. Add garbanzo beans, pecans, and green onions; toss gently.

Cut a piece of aluminum foil long enough to fit around ribs; fold foil lengthwise into thirds. Wrap foil around ribs; fold over tips of ribs. Spoon rice mixture into center of roast; cover with foil. Insert meat thermometer into roast, making sure it does not touch fat or bone. Bake at 325° for 1½ to 2 hours or until meat thermometer registers 160°. Remove foil from roast; let stand 10 minutes before serving. Garnish, if desired. Serve with *Chateau Biltmore Chardonnay Barrel Fermented.* Yield: 12 servings.

Spinach- and Herb-Stuffed Pork

1	(10-ounce) package frozen chopped spinach, thawed and drained
1	(3-ounce) package cream cheese, softened
4	green onions, chopped
¼	cup chopped fresh basil
2 to 3	cloves garlic, finely chopped
1½	teaspoons chopped fresh tarragon
¼	teaspoon ground red pepper
1	(3- to 4-pound) boneless pork loin roast
¼	teaspoon salt
⅛	teaspoon black pepper

Combine first 7 ingredients, stirring well; set aside. Slice roast lengthwise, cutting to but not through one side. Open cut piece to enlarge roast; pound to ½-inch thickness, making a large rectangle. Sprinkle with salt and black pepper. Spoon spinach mixture evenly over pork. Beginning with long side, roll up pork, jellyroll fashion; secure at 2-inch intervals, using heavy string. Place on a greased rack in a shallow roasting pan. Insert meat thermometer into thickest part of roast, making sure it does not touch fat. Bake at 325° for 1 hour and 15 minutes or until meat thermometer registers 160°. Remove from oven; let stand 10 minutes. Remove string; place roast on a serving platter. Serve with *Biltmore Estate Chardonnay sur Lies.* Yield: 10 servings.

Roasted Loin of Pork with Sage and Onion Dressing

1   (4- to 5-pound) center pork loin roast
⅛   teaspoon salt
⅛   teaspoon pepper
1   cup chicken broth
1   tablespoon plus 2 teaspoons all-purpose flour
    Sage and Onion Dressing

Score fat on roast in a diamond design; rub salt and pepper into scored slits and over entire surface of roast. Place roast, fat side up, on a rack in a roasting pan. Insert meat thermometer into thickest part of roast, making sure it does not touch fat or bone. Bake, uncovered, at 325° for 2 hours and 55 minutes or until meat thermometer registers 160°, basting frequently with drippings. Transfer roast to a serving platter; set aside, and keep warm.

Add enough chicken broth to drippings to make 1½ cups. Place in a small heavy saucepan; stir in flour. Cook over medium heat, stirring constantly, until thickened. Accompany roast and gravy with Sage and Onion Dressing. Serve with *Chateau Biltmore Pinot Noir* or *Biltmore Estate Cabernet-Franc.* Yield: 10 to 12 servings.

Sage and Onion Dressing

4½   cups crumbled cornbread
3   cups coarsely crumbled bread
1½   cups finely chopped celery
3   large onions, finely chopped
3   hard-cooked eggs, chopped
2½   cups chicken broth
¾   cup butter or margarine, melted
1½   tablespoons rubbed sage

Combine all ingredients in a large bowl; stir well. Spoon mixture into a greased 13- x 9- x 2-inch baking dish. Bake, uncovered, at 325° for 1 hour and 10 minutes or until golden. Let stand 10 minutes before serving. Yield: 10 to 12 servings.

Olive-Pork Scallopini

½ cup all-purpose flour
½ teaspoon salt
¼ teaspoon pepper
2 (¾-pound) pork tenderloins, cut into ½-inch slices
2 tablespoons vegetable oil
½ cup sliced green onions
½ cup dry sherry
½ cup water
½ teaspoon dried marjoram
½ teaspoon dried basil
2 cups sliced fresh mushrooms
½ cup sliced pimiento-stuffed olives

Combine first 3 ingredients; dredge pork slices in flour mixture. Cook pork slices in hot oil in a large skillet until browned on both sides. Add green onions and next 4 ingredients; bring mixture just to a simmer. Add mushrooms and olives; cook pork 4 minutes on each side or until tender. Serve with *Biltmore Estate Cardinal's Crest* or *Biltmore Estate Merlot.* Yield: 4 to 6 servings.

Ham à l'Orange

3½ cups water
1 (12-ounce) can frozen orange juice concentrate, thawed and undiluted
2 cups firmly packed brown sugar
¼ cup cornstarch
1 teaspoon ground cloves
1 teaspoon ground cinnamon
1 (8-pound) smoked, fully cooked ham half
Whole cloves
1 (11-ounce) can mandarin oranges, drained
Garnish: fresh parsley sprigs, orange slices, whole crabapples

Combine first 6 ingredients in a large saucepan; stir well. Bring to a boil over medium heat, stirring constantly; cook 1 minute, stirring constantly. Reserve 2 cups orange mixture for basting. Set remaining 4 cups aside to serve with ham.

Trim skin from ham. Score fat on ham in a diamond design, and stud with cloves. Place ham, fat side up, on a rack in a shallow roasting pan. Insert meat thermometer, making sure it does not touch fat or bone. Cover and bake at 325° for 1 hour.

Uncover ham; baste with reserved 2 cups orange mixture. Bake, uncovered, for 2½ hours or until meat thermometer registers 140°, basting frequently with orange mixture. Cover with aluminum foil the last 45 minutes of baking to prevent excessive browning, if necessary.

Combine remaining 4 cups orange mixture and mandarin oranges in a saucepan. Cook over medium heat until thoroughly heated, stirring occasionally. Serve with ham. Garnish, if desired. Serve with *Biltmore Estate Johannisberg Riesling.* Yield: 16 servings.

Baked Stuffed Chicken

4 skinned and boned whole chicken breasts
4 (1-ounce) slices baked or smoked ham
4 (1-ounce) slices smoked Gouda cheese
4 large eggs, lightly beaten
½ cup milk
1 teaspoon salt
1 teaspoon ground white pepper
2 cups fine, dry breadcrumbs
1½ teaspoons paprika
1½ cups all-purpose flour
  Poulet Sauce

Place chicken between two sheets of heavy-duty plastic wrap; flatten to ¼-inch thickness, using a meat mallet or rolling pin. Place 1 slice each of ham and cheese in center of each piece of chicken; roll up lengthwise, tucking edges inside. Secure each roll with a wooden pick.

Combine eggs and next 3 ingredients; stir well. Combine breadcrumbs and paprika; stir well. Dredge chicken in flour; dip in egg mixture, and roll in crumb mixture. Place chicken on a greased baking sheet. Bake, uncovered, at 350° for 45 minutes or until done. Accompany with Poulet Sauce. Serve with *Chateau Biltmore Chardonnay Barrel Fermented* or *Biltmore Estate Dry Riesling.* Yield: 4 servings.

Poulet Sauce

2 cups sliced fresh mushrooms
½ cup diced onion
2 tablespoons butter, melted
¼ cup all-purpose flour
½ teaspoon salt
½ teaspoon dried thyme
½ teaspoon freshly ground pepper
2 cups chicken broth

Cook mushrooms and onion in butter in a saucepan over medium heat, stirring constantly, until tender. Add flour and next 3 ingredients; cook over low heat, stirring constantly, 1 minute. Gradually add broth; cook over medium heat, stirring constantly, until mixture is thickened and bubbly. Yield: 2¾ cups.

Chicken Sauté in Puff Pastry

1	(10-ounce) package frozen puff pastry shells
1	medium leek, sliced
1½	pounds skinned and boned chicken breasts, cut into 1-inch pieces
¼	cup butter, melted
½	pound sliced fresh mushrooms
¾	cup whipping cream
¾	cup half-and-half
2	teaspoons chopped fresh parsley
¼	teaspoon salt
⅛	teaspoon freshly ground pepper

Bake pastry shells according to package directions; cool. Pull out and discard center of shells; set shells aside. Remove and discard root, tough outer leaves, and green top from leek. Thinly slice white portion of leek; set aside.

Cook chicken in butter in a large skillet over medium heat, stirring constantly, 5 minutes. Add leek and mushrooms; cook, stirring constantly, 5 minutes. Add cream, half-and-half, and parsley. Cook over medium heat 25 minutes or until thickened, stirring frequently. Stir in salt and pepper. Spoon chicken mixture into pastry shells. Serve with *Biltmore Estate Methode Champenoise "Brut"* or *Biltmore Estate Cardinal's Crest.* Yield: 6 servings.

Le Poulet au Champagne

2 or 3	dried morel mushrooms (about ¼ ounce)
1	(2½- to 3-pound) broiler-fryer, cut up
½	cup butter, melted and divided
2	cups dry champagne
½	cup dry sherry
½	cup chicken broth
¼	cup plus 2 tablespoons whipping cream
⅛	teaspoon salt
⅛	teaspoon pepper

Cover mushrooms with boiling water; let stand 20 minutes. Drain and rinse mushrooms under running water to remove sand particles. Chop mushrooms, and set aside.

Cook chicken in ¼ cup butter in a saucepan over medium heat 10 minutes or until golden, turning to brown all sides. Add mushrooms; cook 2 minutes, stirring frequently. Add champagne, sherry, and broth; bring to a boil. Cover, reduce heat, and simmer 30 minutes or until chicken is done. Transfer chicken to a serving platter, reserving liquid in pan. Keep chicken warm.

Cook reserved liquid over high heat 10 minutes or until liquid is reduced to 1½ cups. Add cream, and cook 5 minutes or until slightly thickened. Whisk in remaining ¼ cup butter, salt, and pepper; cook 2 minutes or until thickened. Spoon over chicken. Serve with *Chateau Biltmore Methode Champenoise "Brut."* Yield: 4 servings.

Cornish Game Hens for Two with Cherry-Mandarin Glaze

2 small sweet potatoes
1 (11-ounce) can mandarin oranges in light syrup, undrained
½ cup chopped pecans
2 tablespoons butter, melted
¼ cup plus 3 tablespoons fresh orange juice
1 tablespoon cornstarch
1 tablespoon brown sugar
2 (1½-pound) Cornish hens
½ cup fresh cherries, pitted and halved

Prick each potato several times with a fork. Microwave, uncovered, at HIGH 5 minutes or until done, turning potatoes after 2½ minutes. Let cool. Peel potatoes; cut into ½-inch cubes.

Drain mandarin oranges, reserving syrup. Combine ½ cup orange segments, potato cubes, pecans, and butter in a bowl; toss gently. Combine reserved syrup, orange juice, cornstarch, and brown sugar in a saucepan; stir well. Bring to a boil, stirring constantly; boil 1 minute. Set aside ¼ cup orange mixture to baste hens; reserve remaining ¾ cup orange mixture for sauce.

Remove giblets from hens; reserve for another use. Rinse hens with cold water, and pat dry. Stuff hens with potato mixture, and close cavities. Secure with wooden picks; truss. Place hens, breast side up, on a rack in a shallow roasting pan. Bake, uncovered, at 350° for 55 minutes. Brush with ¼ cup orange mixture. Bake an additional 10 minutes or until done.

Combine reserved ¾ cup orange mixture, remaining orange segments, and cherries in a saucepan. Cook over medium heat until heated. Spoon ¼ cup sauce over hens. Accompany with remaining sauce. Serve with *Biltmore Estate Cabernet-Sauvignon Blanc de Noir.* Yield: 2 servings.

Turkey Filet Mignon

1 (3-pound) boneless turkey breast, skinned
8 slices bacon
½ cup white wine vinegar
½ cup olive oil
¼ cup chopped fresh basil
1 tablespoon chopped fresh rosemary
½ teaspoon salt
½ teaspoon pepper
Garnish: fresh rosemary sprigs or fresh ramps (wild leeks)

Cut each turkey breast half crosswise into ¾-inch-thick slices. Partially cook bacon, if desired. Wrap one slice of bacon around edge of each slice; secure with a wooden pick. Place turkey slices in a large shallow dish. Combine vinegar and next 5 ingredients; pour over turkey. Cover and marinate in refrigerator 8 hours, turning once. Remove turkey from marinade; discard marinade. Grill turkey, uncovered, over medium-hot coals (350° to 400°) 8 minutes on each side or until done. Garnish, if desired. Serve with *Chateau Biltmore Chardonnay Barrel Fermented.* Yield: 8 servings.

Turkey Filet Mignon, Mushroom Ragoût (page 122), Mushroom-Shaped Truffled Potatoes (page 123), Colorful Vegetable Sauté (page 124)

Braised Grouper with Wild Mushrooms

2	ounces dried morel, cèpe, or porcini mushrooms
¼	cup butter, melted and divided
1	cup finely chopped shallots
1	cup finely chopped fresh mushrooms
½	cup Chardonnay or other dry white wine
	Pinch of dried thyme
4	(6-ounce) grouper fillets (1 inch thick)
½	teaspoon salt
¼	teaspoon pepper
2	cups whipping cream

Cover dried mushrooms with hot water; let stand 30 minutes. Drain and rinse mushrooms under running water to remove sand particles. Slice mushrooms; cook in 2 tablespoons butter in a skillet over medium heat, stirring constantly, 6 to 8 minutes or until tender. Set aside; keep warm.

Cook shallots and chopped mushrooms in remaining 2 tablespoons butter in a medium skillet over medium heat until tender. Add wine and thyme; spoon wine mixture into an 11- x 7- x 1½-inch baking dish.

Sprinkle fillets with salt and pepper; arrange fillets in a single layer over wine mixture in baking dish. Cover and bake at 400° for 20 to 30 minutes or until fish flakes easily when tested with a fork. Transfer fish to a serving platter, and keep warm.

Transfer wine mixture to a saucepan. Cook over medium-high heat 8 minutes or until mixture is reduced to about ½ cup. Add whipping cream; bring to a boil. Reduce heat; simmer, uncovered, 20 to 30 minutes or until thickened. Pour mixture through a wire-mesh strainer into a bowl, discarding shallots and chopped mushrooms. Spoon sliced mushrooms and cream sauce over fish. Serve with *Chateau Biltmore Chardonnay Barrel Fermented* or *Biltmore Estate Chardonnay sur Lies*. Yield: 4 servings.

Tuna Steaks with Tarragon Butter

2	tablespoons butter or margarine, softened
¼	teaspoon lemon juice
½	teaspoon minced fresh tarragon or ¼ teaspoon dried tarragon
2	(8-ounce) tuna steaks (about ¾ inch thick)
¼	teaspoon salt
¼	teaspoon freshly ground pepper
1	tablespoon olive oil

Combine butter, lemon juice, and tarragon; stir well. Shape into a 1-inch-diameter log; cover and chill until firm.

Sprinkle tuna with salt and pepper. Cook tuna in hot oil in a nonstick skillet over medium heat 5 minutes on each side or to desired degree of doneness.

Slice and serve tarragon butter with tuna. Serve with *Biltmore Estate Sauvignon Blanc* or *Biltmore Estate Chardonnay sur Lies*. Yield: 2 servings.

Layered Salmon-and-Spinach Terrine

1	pound fresh spinach
6	green onions, finely chopped
3	tablespoons butter or margarine, melted
1½	pounds sole fillets or other fish fillets, cut into 2-inch pieces
2	cups lightly packed, finely crumbled French bread
2	cups whipping cream
2	large eggs
¼	cup lemon juice
1	teaspoon salt
¼	teaspoon ground white pepper
¼	teaspoon ground nutmeg
8	ounces smoked salmon
1	(8-ounce) carton sour cream
2	teaspoons Dijon mustard
1	teaspoon lemon juice
½	teaspoon salt
	Dash of ground white pepper
	Garnish: small fresh spinach leaves

Remove stems from spinach; wash leaves thoroughly, and pat dry. Finely chop leaves. Cook spinach and green onions in butter in a large skillet over medium-high heat, stirring constantly, until spinach wilts. Set aside.

Position knife blade in food processor bowl; add half of sole. Process 45 seconds or until smooth. Add half of bread and half of each of next 6 ingredients to processor bowl; process 30 seconds or until smooth. (Mixture will be soft but will hold its shape.) Transfer to a large bowl. Repeat procedure with remaining sole, bread, cream, egg, lemon juice, and seasonings. Stir sole mixtures together. Spread 1 cup of sole mixture in a buttered 9- x 5- x 3-inch loafpan.

Place salmon and 1 cup sole mixture in processor bowl; process 30 seconds or just until mixture is smooth. Carefully spread salmon mixture over first layer. Spread 1 cup sole mixture over second layer. Combine spinach mixture and 2 cups sole mixture; spread spinach mixture over third layer. Spread remaining sole mixture over spinach layer.

Cover top of terrine with buttered wax paper cut just larger than the top of pan. Fit aluminum foil over wax paper and top of pan; crimp tightly to top of pan. (Do not cover sides of pan with foil.) Carefully prick holes through foil and wax paper in several places to allow steam to escape.

Place loafpan in a 13- x 9- x 2-inch baking pan; add hot water to larger pan to depth of 1 inch. Bake at 350° for 1 hour and 15 minutes to 1 hour and 25 minutes or until terrine starts to rise above rim of loafpan and top is firm and springy to the touch. Remove from oven; remove foil and wax paper, and cool, draining off pan drippings as terrine cools. Cool completely; cover and chill 8 hours.

Combine sour cream and next 4 ingredients, stirring well; cover and chill thoroughly.

Invert terrine onto a serving platter; let stand at room temperature 30 minutes. Slice with an electric knife. To serve, spoon sour cream mixture evenly on individual plates; place terrine slices over mixture, and garnish, if desired. Serve with *Biltmore Estate Sauvignon Blanc* or *Biltmore Estate Chardonnay sur Lies*. Yield: 15 to 18 servings.

Crab, Shrimp, and Artichoke au Gratin

    4   cups water
    1   pound unpeeled medium-size fresh shrimp
    1   (9-ounce) package frozen artichoke hearts
    ¾   pound fresh lump crabmeat, drained
    2   cups (8 ounces) shredded sharp Cheddar cheese, divided
    ½   pound fresh mushrooms, sliced
    2   tablespoons sliced green onions
    1   clove garlic, minced
    2   tablespoons butter or margarine, melted
    ¼   cup butter or margarine
    ¼   cup all-purpose flour
    ¾   cup half-and-half
    1   tablespoon chopped fresh dillweed or 1 teaspoon dried dillweed
    ½   teaspoon pepper
    ⅔   cup dry white wine
    2   tablespoons corn flake crumbs
    1½ teaspoons butter or margarine, melted

Bring water to a boil; add shrimp, and cook 3 to 5 minutes. Drain well; rinse with cold water. Peel and devein shrimp; set aside.

Cook artichoke hearts according to package directions; drain. Combine artichokes, shrimp, crabmeat, and 1 cup cheese in a large bowl; set aside.

Cook mushrooms, green onions, and garlic in 2 tablespoons butter in a skillet over medium-high heat, stirring constantly, until tender; drain. Add mushroom mixture to shrimp mixture.

Melt ¼ cup butter in a large heavy skillet over low heat; add flour, stirring until smooth. Cook 1 minute, stirring constantly. Gradually add half-and-half; cook over medium heat, stirring constantly, until thickened and bubbly. Remove from heat; stir in dillweed, pepper, and remaining 1 cup cheese, stirring until cheese melts. Gradually stir in wine. Cook sauce over medium heat, stirring constantly, until thickened. Add shrimp mixture, stirring well. Spoon into a lightly greased 2-quart shallow baking dish; cover and chill 8 hours.

To serve, remove from refrigerator, and let stand at room temperature 30 minutes. Combine corn flake crumbs and 1½ teaspoons melted butter; sprinkle over casserole. Bake, uncovered, at 350° for 45 minutes. Serve with *Biltmore Estate Methode Champenoise "Brut"* or *Biltmore Estate Sauvignon Blanc.* Yield: 6 to 8 servings.

Shrimp with Asparagus en Papillote

2 to 3	tablespoons vegetable oil
1½	pounds fresh asparagus
¼	cup butter or margarine, softened
2	tablespoons peeled, grated gingerroot
2	teaspoons grated lemon rind
1½	tablespoons fresh lemon juice
¼	teaspoon salt
1	large clove garlic, crushed
2	pounds unpeeled medium-size fresh shrimp
6	lemon slices

Cut 6 (15- x 12-inch) rectangles of parchment paper or aluminum foil. Fold each in half lengthwise; trim into large heart shapes. Place on baking sheets; open out flat. Lightly brush one half of each heart with oil, leaving edges ungreased.

Snap off tough ends of asparagus. Arrange asparagus in a steamer over boiling water; cover and steam 3 minutes. Drain and rinse in cold water; drain. Stir together butter and next 5 ingredients; set aside.

Peel and devein shrimp. Arrange asparagus evenly on greased half of each heart near the crease; arrange shrimp over asparagus. Dot with butter mixture; top each with a lemon slice. Fold over paper edges. Starting with rounded edge of each heart, pleat and crimp edges together to make an airtight seal. Bake at 400° for 9 to 11 minutes or until bags are puffed and lightly browned and shrimp turn pink. Serve with *Chateau Biltmore Chardonnay Barrel Fermented.* Yield: 6 servings.

Oysters au Gratin

2	(12-ounce) containers fresh Standard oysters, undrained
2	cups saltine cracker crumbs, divided
⅔	cup grated Parmesan cheese
½	teaspoon salt
¼	teaspoon black pepper
¾	cup half-and-half
½	cup butter or margarine, melted
¼	cup dry white wine
1	tablespoon anchovy paste
½	teaspoon grated lemon rind
⅛	teaspoon ground red pepper

Drain oysters, reserving ⅓ cup liquid. Set aside.

Sprinkle ½ cup cracker crumbs in a lightly greased 8-inch square baking dish. Layer half each of oysters, remaining cracker crumbs, cheese, salt, and black pepper in dish. Repeat layers.

Combine reserved oyster liquid, half-and-half, and remaining ingredients; stir well. Pour over oyster mixture. Bake, uncovered, at 350° for 35 minutes or until golden. Serve with *Biltmore Estate Methode Champenoise "Brut"* or *Biltmore Estate Sauvignon Blanc.* Yield: 6 servings.

Roasted Duckling with Orange Sauce

1 (4- to 4½-pound) dressed duckling
¼ cup butter or margarine, divided
¼ teaspoon salt
¼ teaspoon pepper
4 slices bacon
1 tablespoon all-purpose flour
Orange Sauce

Remove giblets from duckling; reserve for another use. Rinse duckling with cold water, and pat dry. Prick skin with a fork at 2-inch intervals. Place 2 tablespoons butter in cavity; sprinkle cavity with salt and pepper.

Place duckling, breast side up, in a lightly greased roasting pan. Melt remaining 2 tablespoons butter, and brush over duckling. Arrange bacon slices in a crisscross pattern over duckling. Insert meat thermometer into thigh, making sure it does not touch bone. Bake at 400° for 30 to 35 minutes, basting frequently with drippings. Remove and discard bacon. Sprinkle duckling with flour; baste well. Reduce heat to 325°, and bake 2 hours or until meat thermometer registers 180°. Cover duckling loosely with aluminum foil to prevent overbrowning, if necessary. Remove duckling to a serving platter. Accompany with Orange Sauce. Serve with *Chateau Biltmore Merlot* or *Chateau Biltmore Cabernet-Franc.* Yield: 4 to 6 servings.

Orange Sauce

1 small onion, sliced
1 tablespoon butter or margarine, melted
4 (2- x ¼-inch) orange rind strips
1 cup fresh orange juice
¼ cup port wine
⅛ teaspoon pepper
2 teaspoons cornstarch
1 tablespoon water

Cook onion in butter in a small saucepan over medium-high heat, stirring constantly, until tender; add orange rind and orange juice. Bring to a boil; reduce heat, and simmer, uncovered, 10 minutes. Strain orange juice mixture, discarding onion and orange rind. Combine orange juice mixture, wine, and pepper; stir well.

Combine cornstarch and water; stir well. Stir into orange juice mixture. Bring to a boil, stirring constantly, over medium heat; cook 1 minute. Yield: about 1 cup.

Goose Ragoût

1	(9- to 10-pound) dressed goose
1	teaspoon salt
½	teaspoon pepper
2	stalks celery, coarsely chopped
1	medium onion, quartered
1	cooking apple, quartered
1	medium onion, chopped
4	cloves garlic, minced
2	tablespoons olive oil
1	(14½-ounce) can Italian-style tomatoes, undrained and chopped
1	teaspoon salt
½	teaspoon sugar
1	teaspoon dried rosemary
½	teaspoon dried thyme
1½	cups dry red wine
2	cups beef broth
1	tablespoon white wine vinegar
2	cups scraped, sliced carrot
2	cups peeled, chopped potato
1	cup pearl onions, peeled
½	cup water
2	tablespoons all-purpose flour

Remove giblets and neck from goose; reserve for another use. Rinse goose thoroughly with water; pat dry. Prick skin with a fork at 2-inch intervals; rub with 1 teaspoon salt and pepper. Stuff cavity of goose with celery, quartered onion, and apple; close cavity with skewers. Truss goose, and place, breast side up, on a rack in a roasting pan. Insert meat thermometer in thigh, making sure it does not touch bone. Bake, uncovered, at 350° for 2 to 2½ hours or until meat thermometer registers 180°. Remove from oven; let cool. Remove and shred meat; set aside.

Cook chopped onion and garlic in hot oil in a large Dutch oven over medium-high heat, stirring constantly, until tender. Add tomato and next 4 ingredients; stir well. Add wine, broth, and vinegar; bring to a boil. Cover, reduce heat, and simmer 15 minutes. Add carrot, potato, and pearl onions; cover and simmer 20 minutes. Add meat; cover and simmer 30 minutes.

Combine water and flour, stirring until smooth. Add flour mixture to meat mixture; cook over medium heat until thickened, stirring occasionally. Serve with *Chateau Biltmore Pinot Noir* or *Biltmore Estate Merlot*. Yield: 3 quarts.

Fruit-Stuffed Wild Goose

1	(4- to 5-pound) dressed wild goose
½	teaspoon salt
⅛	teaspoon pepper
6	slices bacon
1	cup sliced green onions
¼	cup chopped green pepper
1	(8-ounce) package herb-seasoned stuffing mix
1¼	cups water
1	cup chopped dried apricots
½	cup chopped pitted dates
1	large egg, lightly beaten
	Garnish: fresh sage, fresh thyme, fresh rosemary, dried apricot roses

Remove giblets and neck from goose; reserve for another use. Rinse goose thoroughly with cold water; pat dry. Sprinkle salt and pepper inside cavity of goose.

Cook bacon in a skillet until crisp; remove bacon, reserving drippings in skillet. Crumble bacon. Cook green onions and green pepper in drippings, stirring constantly, until crisp-tender.

Combine bacon, green onion mixture, stuffing mix, and next 4 ingredients. Spoon into goose cavity; close cavity with skewers. Truss goose; place, breast side up, on a rack in a roasting pan. Insert meat thermometer in thigh, making sure it does not touch bone. Bake, uncovered, at 350° for 1 hour and 45 minutes or until meat thermometer registers 180°. Spoon any remaining stuffing mixture into a lightly greased baking dish; cover and bake at 350° for 40 minutes or until done. Garnish, if desired. Serve with *Chateau Biltmore Cabernet-Sauvignon*. Yield: 4 to 6 servings.

Baked Quail with Mushrooms

⅓	cup all-purpose flour
½	teaspoon salt
½	teaspoon pepper
8	quail
½	pound fresh mushrooms, sliced
½	cup butter or margarine, melted and divided
¼	cup plus 1 tablespoon all-purpose flour
2	cups chicken broth
½	cup dry sherry

Combine first 3 ingredients. Dredge quail in flour mixture, and set aside.

Cook mushrooms in 2 tablespoons butter in a large skillet over medium-high heat, stirring constantly, 4 minutes. Remove mushrooms from skillet; drain and set aside.

Brown quail on both sides in remaining ¼ cup plus 2 tablespoons butter in skillet. Transfer quail to a 1½-quart casserole. Add ¼ cup plus 1 tablespoon flour to drippings in skillet; cook 1 minute, stirring constantly. Gradually add chicken broth and sherry; cook over medium heat, stirring constantly, until thickened. Stir in mushrooms; pour over quail. Cover and bake at 350° for 1 hour. Serve with *Chateau Biltmore Merlot*. Yield: 4 servings.

Pheasant Soup

1   cup diced celery
1   medium leek, halved lengthwise and sliced
1   tablespoon olive oil
1½   quarts Pheasant Stock
5   chicken-flavored bouillon cubes
½   teaspoon ground white pepper
½   teaspoon dried onion flakes
½   teaspoon dried thyme
1   bay leaf
4   ounces fresh oyster mushrooms, sliced
¼   cup sherry
¼   cup plus 2 tablespoons butter
¼   cup plus 2 tablespoons all-purpose flour
     Diced pheasant meat (from Pheasant Stock)
½   cup half-and-half

Cook celery and leek in hot oil in a Dutch oven over medium heat until tender. Add Pheasant Stock and next 5 ingredients. Bring to a boil; cover, reduce heat, and simmer 1 hour. Skim off any foam or fat, if necessary.

Combine mushrooms and sherry in a small saucepan; bring to a boil. Reduce heat, and cook 5 minutes or until mushrooms are tender; set aside. Melt butter in a medium skillet; add flour, and cook over medium heat, stirring constantly, 5 minutes (do not let brown). Set roux aside.

Add mushrooms and pheasant meat to Dutch oven; stir well. Add roux; bring to a boil. Reduce heat, and simmer 8 to 10 minutes or until slightly thickened, stirring occasionally. Remove and discard bay leaf. Stir in half-and-half, and cook over low heat until thoroughly heated. Serve with *Chateau Biltmore Cabernet-Sauvignon.* Yield: 2 quarts.

Pheasant Stock

1   (2½-pound) pheasant
3   quarts water
1   stalk celery, cut into 2-inch pieces
1   carrot, scraped and cut into 2-inch pieces
1   small onion, quartered
½   teaspoon cracked black pepper
½   teaspoon dried thyme
2   whole cloves
1   bay leaf

Combine all ingredients in a Dutch oven. Bring to a boil; cover, reduce heat, and simmer 45 minutes or until pheasant is tender. Remove pheasant from stock, reserving stock; let cool to touch. Remove skin; bone pheasant, and dice meat. Set aside for soup. Return bones to stock. Bring stock to a boil; cook 20 to 25 minutes or until mixture is reduced by one-fourth. Strain stock through a cheesecloth- or paper towel-lined sieve into a bowl. Discard vegetables, bay leaf, and cloves. Yield: 2 quarts.

Broiled Pigeon

2	squab (pigeons), split in half lengthwise (about 1½ pounds)
3	tablespoons butter or margarine, melted
½	cup all-purpose flour
½	teaspoon salt
¼	teaspoon pepper
3	tablespoons butter or margarine, melted
1	tablespoon Worcestershire sauce
⅓	cup dry white wine
4	(¾-inch-thick) slices French bread
1	tablespoon butter or margarine, softened
¼	teaspoon garlic salt
⅛	teaspoon pepper
	Red Plum Sauce

Brush squab with 3 tablespoons melted butter. Combine flour, salt, and ¼ teaspoon pepper; dredge squab in flour mixture.

Cook squab in 3 tablespoons butter in a large skillet over medium heat, turning to brown all sides. Place squab in a greased 9-inch square pan, and brush with Worcestershire sauce; pour wine into pan. Cover and bake at 400° for 35 minutes; uncover and bake an additional 10 minutes or until squab is tender.

Place bread slices on a baking sheet; spread 1 tablespoon softened butter evenly over slices. Sprinkle slices evenly with garlic salt and ⅛ teaspoon pepper. Broil 5½ inches from heat (with electric oven door partially opened) 2 minutes or until toasted.

Place 1 squab half on each slice of toast; accompany with Red Plum Sauce. Serve with *Chateau Biltmore Vanderbilt Claret* or *Chateau Biltmore Cabernet-Sauvignon.* Yield: 4 servings.

Red Plum Sauce

⅔	cup red plum jam
½	teaspoon grated orange rind
½	teaspoon grated lemon rind
⅓	cup fresh orange juice
2	tablespoons lemon juice
2	teaspoons cornstarch
¼	teaspoon dry mustard

Combine all ingredients in a medium saucepan; stir well. Bring to a boil over medium heat, stirring constantly, until thickened and bubbly. Serve warm. Yield: 1 cup.

Rabbit à l'Italienne

1	clove garlic, halved
3	tablespoons olive oil
1	(3-pound) rabbit, dressed and cut up
3	cups dry white wine
½	teaspoon coarsely ground pepper
¼	teaspoon ground coriander
2	sprigs fresh rosemary
2	shallots, sliced
2	teaspoons anchovy paste
2	teaspoons drained capers
3	tablespoons butter or margarine, melted
3	tablespoons all-purpose flour
2	tablespoons beef-flavored bouillon granules
1	cup water
1	teaspoon salt
¼	teaspoon coarsely ground pepper
	Hot cooked rice
	Garnish: fresh rosemary sprigs

Rub cut side of garlic over bottom and sides of a large Dutch oven; add oil. Brown rabbit in hot oil over medium-high heat. Add wine and next 3 ingredients. Bring to a boil; reduce heat, and simmer, uncovered, 40 minutes. Transfer rabbit to a serving dish, and keep warm. Pour liquid through a wire-mesh strainer into a bowl; set aside.

Cook shallots, anchovy paste, and capers in butter in a large skillet until butter begins to brown, stirring frequently. Add flour, stirring until smooth; cook, stirring constantly, 1 minute. Add bouillon granules and water; stir in reserved liquid. Cook over medium heat, stirring constantly, until thickened and bubbly; stir in salt and ¼ teaspoon pepper. Spoon sauce over rabbit; accompany with hot cooked rice. Garnish, if desired. Serve with *Biltmore Estate "Nouveau" Red* or *Biltmore Estate Cardinal's Crest*. Yield: 4 to 6 servings.

Rabbit and Wild Rice Soup

1   (6-ounce) package long-grain and wild rice mix
     Cubed rabbit meat (from Rabbit Stock)
1   tablespoon vegetable oil
2   quarts Rabbit Stock
¼   cup cornstarch
¼   cup water

Cook rice mix according to package directions; set 2 cups rice aside. Reserve remaining rice for another use.

Brown rabbit meat in hot oil in a large Dutch oven over medium-high heat. Add Rabbit Stock; bring to a boil. Cover, reduce heat, and simmer 20 minutes. Stir in 2 cups cooked rice. Combine cornstarch and water, stirring until smooth; add to stock mixture. Cook over medium heat, stirring constantly, until slightly thickened. Serve with *Biltmore Estate Dry Riesling* or *Biltmore Estate Sauvignon Blanc.* Yield: 2¼ quarts.

Rabbit Stock

1   skinned rabbit (about 2½ pounds)
1   cup sliced leeks
1   cup sliced shiitake mushrooms
1   cup diced celery
1   cup diced carrot
2   gallons water
1 to 1½ teaspoons salt
½   teaspoon pepper
¼   teaspoon onion powder
2   cloves garlic, pressed
1   bay leaf

Debone rabbit, reserving bones and meat. Cube meat; set aside for soup.

Combine leeks and next 3 ingredients in a 13- x 9- x 2-inch baking dish. Place rabbit bones over vegetable mixture. Bake, uncovered, at 400° for 25 to 30 minutes or until bones are browned.

Place browned bones and vegetable mixture in a large stockpot. Add 2 gallons water and remaining ingredients; bring to a boil. Cook over high heat 3½ hours or until mixture is reduced to 3 quarts. Strain stock into a bowl, discarding bones, vegetables, and bay leaf. Yield: 2 quarts.

Stewed Venison

2	pounds boneless venison, cut into ½-inch pieces
½	cup all-purpose flour
¼	cup bacon drippings
12	small boiling onions
4	carrots, cut into ½-inch slices
½	cup sliced fresh mushrooms
2	shallots, chopped
2	cups dry red wine
3	cups beef broth
1	(10½-ounce) can French onion soup
½	teaspoon pepper
¼	teaspoon salt
2	cloves garlic, minced
2	bay leaves
	Hot cooked rice or biscuits (optional)

Dredge venison in flour; cook venison in hot bacon drippings in a large Dutch oven over medium heat until browned, turning frequently. Add onions and next 10 ingredients. Bring to a boil; cover, reduce heat, and simmer 2 hours, stirring occasionally. Remove and discard bay leaves. Spoon over rice or biscuits, if desired. Serve with *Biltmore Estate Cabernet-Sauvignon* or *Chateau Biltmore Cabernet-Sauvignon.* Yield: 8 to 10 servings.

Side Dishes

Cranberry Waldorf Salad with Chantilly Dressing

3	cups fresh cranberries, coarsely chopped
1½	cups sugar
1½	cups unpeeled, diced Red Delicious apple
1½	cups halved, seedless green grapes
1½	cups fresh orange sections (about 3 large)
¾	cup chopped walnuts, toasted
½	cup whipping cream, whipped
½	cup mayonnaise
1½	tablespoons powdered sugar

Combine cranberries and 1½ cups sugar, stirring well. Place mixture in a colander or sieve. Place colander in a large bowl; cover and chill at least 8 hours.

Transfer cranberry mixture to a large bowl; discard liquid. Add apple, grapes, orange sections, and walnuts to cranberry mixture; toss lightly. Spoon mixture evenly onto individual salad plates.

Combine whipped cream, mayonnaise, and powdered sugar; stir gently. Top salads evenly with dressing. Yield: 6 servings.

Pineapple-Rum Ambrosia Salad

3	cups pineapple juice
¼	cup plus 2 tablespoons light rum
¼	cup firmly packed brown sugar
¼	teaspoon ground cloves
3	tablespoons cornstarch
¼	cup water
5	(20-ounce) cans pineapple chunks, drained
1	(16-ounce) jar maraschino cherries, drained and rinsed
2	cups flaked coconut
1	cup chopped dates

Combine first 4 ingredients in a medium saucepan; stir well. Combine cornstarch and water, stirring well; add to juice mixture. Bring to a boil over medium heat, stirring constantly, until mixture is thickened. Remove from heat, and set aside.

Combine pineapple chunks and remaining ingredients in a large bowl. Pour thickened juice mixture over fruit, and stir well. Cover and chill thoroughly. Yield: 12 servings.

Simple Caesar Salad

¼ cup water
1 clove garlic
⅛ teaspoon salt
1 tablespoon white wine vinegar
½ teaspoon Dijon mustard
¼ cup olive oil
2 cups firmly packed torn romaine lettuce
2 tablespoons freshly grated Parmesan cheese
2 tablespoons pine nuts, toasted
⅛ teaspoon freshly ground pepper

Place water and garlic in a small saucepan; bring to a boil. Cover, reduce heat, and simmer 10 minutes or until garlic is soft; drain. Place garlic in a salad bowl; add salt. Mash into a paste, using the back of a spoon. Stir in vinegar and mustard with a wire whisk. Add oil in a slow, steady stream, beating with whisk until well blended. Add lettuce, and toss gently. Sprinkle with cheese, pine nuts, and pepper. Yield: 2 servings.

Salade des Iles

6 spears hearts of palm
Romaine lettuce leaves
1 medium-size sweet red pepper, seeded and cut into very thin strips
Curly endive
6 medium mushroom caps, sliced
Creamy Herb Dressing
1 (8-ounce) can pineapple chunks in juice, drained

Cut lengthwise slits in each heart of palm spear to within ½-inch of one end; fan hearts of palm on lettuce-lined salad plates. Place 1 red pepper strip between each strip of heart of palm fan. Place endive at uncut ends of fans; arrange mushrooms around endive. Just before serving, drizzle Creamy Herb Dressing over each salad; top each with pineapple chunks. Yield: 6 servings.

Creamy Herb Dressing

1 cup mayonnaise
½ cup sour cream
⅓ cup buttermilk
½ teaspoon dried tarragon
⅛ teaspoon dried basil
⅛ teaspoon dried marjoram
⅛ teaspoon garlic powder
⅛ teaspoon ground white pepper

Combine all ingredients; beat with a wire whisk until blended. Cover; chill. Yield: 1¾ cups.

Basil and Tomato Salad with Black Pepper Goat Cheese

     2   tablespoons chopped fresh parsley
     2   tablespoons cracked black pepper
     2   (3-ounce) packages chèvre (goat) cheese
     1   head Bibb lettuce
     6   plum tomatoes, cut into 5 slices each
    12   calamata olives
     1   medium bunch fresh basil
         Herbed Vinaigrette

Combine parsley and pepper; roll cheese in parsley mixture until coated on all sides. Wrap coated cheese logs in heavy-duty plastic wrap; freeze. (This prevents cheese from crumbling when sliced.) Carefully slice each cheese log into 6 (½-inch) slices.

Divide lettuce among 6 salad plates. Fan 5 tomato slices in center of each lettuce-lined plate. Place 2 slices of cheese and 2 olives at base of each tomato fan. Top each with fresh basil. Serve with Herbed Vinaigrette. Yield: 6 servings.

Herbed Vinaigrette

     2   cups olive oil
    ¾   cup balsamic vinegar
     1   (3½-ounce) jar capers, drained
     1   tablespoon chopped fresh oregano
     1   tablespoon chopped fresh tarragon
     1   tablespoon chopped fresh chives
     1   tablespoon minced garlic
    ½   teaspoon salt
    ½   teaspoon sugar
    ¼   teaspoon dried crushed red pepper
    ¼   teaspoon black pepper

Combine all ingredients in a large jar; cover tightly, and shake vigorously. Yield: 3 cups.

German Potato Salad

2   pounds small red potatoes, cut into ¼-inch slices
½   pound kielbasa, cut diagonally into ¼-inch slices
1   small purple onion, diced
     Hot Bacon Dressing

Cook potato slices in boiling water to cover 9 minutes or until tender; drain. Combine potato slices, sausage slices, and onion in a large bowl; toss well. Pour Hot Bacon Dressing over potato mixture, tossing gently to coat. Serve warm. Yield: 8 to 10 servings.

Hot Bacon Dressing

½   pound uncooked bacon, chopped
1   small onion, diced
¾   cup diced celery
1⅔   cups cider vinegar
1¼   cups sugar
1½   tablespoons Dijon mustard
1   teaspoon garlic powder
½   teaspoon dry mustard
¼   teaspoon ground white pepper
1   tablespoon plus 1 teaspoon cornstarch
1   tablespoon plus 1 teaspoon water

Cook bacon in a skillet until crisp; remove bacon, reserving 3 tablespoons drippings in skillet. Return bacon to skillet. Add onion and celery; cook, stirring constantly, until tender. Stir in vinegar. Bring to a boil, and cook 6 minutes or until reduced to 1¼ cups. Add sugar and next 4 ingredients; cook, stirring constantly, until sugar dissolves. Combine cornstarch and water in a bowl; add cornstarch mixture to skillet. Cook over medium heat, stirring constantly, until thickened and bubbly. Serve with German Potato Salad or salad greens. Yield: 2 cups.

Wild Rice with Pecans

2   tablespoons butter or margarine
2   (6-ounce) packages long-grain and wild rice mix
4   cups chicken broth
8   green onions, chopped
8   medium mushrooms, sliced
1½   cups chopped pecans, toasted

Melt butter in a large Dutch oven. Add rice; cook over medium heat until lightly browned, stirring frequently. Stir in rice mix seasoning packets, broth, green onions, and mushrooms. Bring to a boil; remove from heat. Transfer mixture to a lightly greased 3-quart casserole. Cover and bake at 350° for 30 minutes. Uncover and bake an additional 30 minutes or until rice is tender and liquid is absorbed, stirring after 15 minutes. Stir in pecans. Yield: 12 servings.

Orange-Herb Rice

2	tablespoons chopped onion
2	tablespoons butter or margarine, melted
2	cups water
½	teaspoon grated orange rind
½	cup orange juice
1	teaspoon salt
⅛	teaspoon dried marjoram
⅛	teaspoon dried thyme
1	cup long-grain rice, uncooked

Cook onion in butter in a large saucepan over medium-high heat, stirring constantly, until tender. Add water and next 5 ingredients; bring to a boil. Add rice, and stir well. Cover and bring to a boil; reduce heat, and simmer 20 minutes. Yield: 4 to 6 servings.

Spinach Pesto Pasta

1	(10-ounce) package frozen chopped spinach, thawed
½	cup grated Parmesan cheese
½	cup olive oil
⅓	cup fresh basil leaves
¼	cup pine nuts, toasted
2	tablespoons butter or margarine, softened
1	teaspoon crushed garlic
½	teaspoon coarsely ground pepper
¼	teaspoon salt
¼	teaspoon anise seed, ground
1	(12-ounce) package egg noodles, uncooked
	Garnish: fresh basil sprigs

Drain spinach; press between paper towels to remove excess moisture. Position knife blade in food processor bowl; add spinach and next 9 ingredients. Process 30 seconds, scraping sides of processor bowl once. Set pesto aside.

Cook noodles according to package directions; drain well. Add pesto to hot noodles, tossing gently. Transfer to a serving bowl; garnish, if desired. Serve immediately. Yield: 8 to 10 servings.

Marmalade Fruit Bake

¾ cup orange marmalade
½ cup orange juice
2 teaspoons cornstarch
1½ teaspoons minced fresh mint leaves
2 (16-ounce) cans pear halves, drained
2 (16-ounce) cans peach halves, drained
1 (11-ounce) can mandarin oranges, drained
Garnishes: fresh mint sprigs, orange curls

Combine first 4 ingredients in a small saucepan; stir well. Bring to a boil; boil 1 minute or until slightly thickened. Remove from heat, and set aside.

Place fruit in a lightly greased 11- x 7- x 1½-inch baking dish; pour marmalade mixture over fruit. Bake, uncovered, at 325° for 20 minutes or until thoroughly heated. Spoon fruit mixture into a serving bowl; garnish, if desired. Serve warm. Yield: 8 servings.

Cheese Pudding

3 tablespoons butter or margarine
3 tablespoons all-purpose flour
1 cup milk
1 cup (4 ounces) shredded Cheddar cheese
2 large eggs, separated

Melt butter in a heavy saucepan over low heat; add flour, stirring until smooth. Cook 1 minute, stirring constantly. Gradually add milk; cook over medium heat, stirring constantly, until thickened and bubbly. Remove from heat; add cheese, stirring until cheese melts.

Beat egg yolks until thick and pale. Gradually stir about one-fourth of hot cheese mixture into yolks; add to remaining hot mixture, stirring constantly. Let cool.

Beat egg whites at high speed of an electric mixer until stiff peaks form; gently fold beaten egg white into cheese mixture. Pour mixture into a lightly buttered 1½-quart soufflé dish. Bake at 350° for 30 minutes or until puffed and golden. Serve immediately. Yield: 6 servings.

Asparagus with Orange Sauce

1½   pounds fresh asparagus spears
1½   teaspoons cornstarch
¼   cup orange juice
2   tablespoons grated orange rind
⅓   cup butter or margarine
¼   teaspoon white pepper
    Garnish: orange slices

Snap off tough ends of asparagus. Remove scales from stalks with a knife or vegetable peeler, if desired. Cook asparagus, covered, in a small amount of boiling water 6 to 8 minutes or until crisp-tender. Drain. Arrange on serving platter; keep warm.

Combine cornstarch and orange juice in a small saucepan; add orange rind, butter, and pepper. Bring mixture to a boil; reduce heat, and cook, stirring constantly, 7 minutes or until mixture thickens slightly. Spoon sauce over asparagus; garnish, if desired. Yield: 4 to 6 servings.

Broccoli with Parmesan Cheese

1¼   pounds fresh broccoli
1   cup water
1   teaspoon salt, divided
¼   teaspoon pepper
¼   teaspoon ground nutmeg
1   cup freshly grated Parmesan cheese
¼   cup fine, dry breadcrumbs
2   tablespoons butter, melted

Wash and trim broccoli; cut into flowerets with 2½-inch stems. (Reserve stems for another use.)

Combine water and ½ teaspoon salt in a large saucepan; bring to a boil. Add broccoli; cover and cook over medium heat 6 minutes or until crisp-tender. Drain and coarsely chop broccoli.

Place half of broccoli in a greased 1½-quart baking dish. Combine remaining ½ teaspoon salt, pepper, and nutmeg; stir well. Sprinkle half of spice mixture over broccoli; top with half of cheese. Repeat layers with remaining broccoli, spice mixture, and cheese.

Combine breadcrumbs and melted butter; sprinkle over cheese layer. Bake, uncovered, at 350° for 15 minutes or until thoroughly heated. Yield: 6 servings.

Glazed Carrots

    1   pound carrots, scraped and cut into ¼-inch slices
    3   tablespoons butter
    ⅓   cup sugar
    ¼   teaspoon salt
    ⅛   teaspoon pepper
    ⅛   teaspoon ground mace

Cook carrot slices in boiling water to cover 6 minutes. Drain and set aside.

Melt butter in a small saucepan over medium heat; stir in sugar and remaining ingredients. Add carrot slices, and bring to a boil. Cover, reduce heat, and simmer 3 to 4 minutes or until carrot is crisp-tender. Uncover and cook over medium-high heat 8 minutes or until butter mixture is reduced and carrot slices are glazed. Yield: 4 servings.

Creamy Corn Pudding

    3   cups fresh corn, cut from cob (3 to 4 ears)
    3   cups whipping cream
    ½   cup sugar
    1   tablespoon butter or margarine, melted
    1   teaspoon all-purpose flour
    ¾   teaspoon salt
    ½   teaspoon baking powder
    6   large eggs, lightly beaten

Position knife blade in food processor bowl; add corn. Process until corn is finely chopped. Place corn in a colander; let drain 1 hour.

Combine drained corn, whipping cream, and remaining ingredients; stir well. Pour mixture into an ungreased 2-quart casserole. Bake, uncovered, at 325° for 1 hour and 45 minutes or until set. Let stand 10 minutes before serving. Yield: 8 servings.

Fried Onions

    1½   pounds onions (about 4 medium), thinly sliced
    ½   cup water
    ¼   cup bacon drippings
    ½   teaspoon salt
    ¼   teaspoon pepper

Cook onion and water in a large skillet over medium heat 10 minutes or until water evaporates. Add bacon drippings, salt, and pepper; stir well. Cook over medium-high heat, stirring frequently, 8 minutes or until onion is tender and lightly browned. Yield: 4 servings.

Boiled Mushrooms in Cream

1	pound fresh mushrooms
⅓	cup finely chopped onion
2	tablespoons chopped fresh parsley
½	cup butter or margarine, melted
2½	tablespoons all-purpose flour
1	cup whipping cream
⅓	cup dry white wine
½	teaspoon salt
¼	teaspoon pepper

Cook first 3 ingredients in butter in a large skillet over medium heat, stirring constantly, until tender. Remove mushrooms, reserving drippings in skillet. Stir flour into drippings. Cook, stirring constantly, 1 minute. Gradually add cream and wine; cook, stirring constantly, until thickened and bubbly. Stir in mushrooms, salt, and pepper; cook until thoroughly heated. Yield: 6 servings.

Mushroom Ragoût

½	pound fresh crimini mushrooms
½	pound fresh shiitake mushrooms
½	pound fresh portabella mushrooms
½	pound fresh oyster mushrooms
1	large clove garlic, crushed
2	tablespoons butter or margarine, melted
1 to 2	tablespoons grated Parmesan cheese
¼	teaspoon pepper
1 to 2	tablespoons soy sauce
	Garnish: fresh enoki mushrooms

Remove and discard mushroom stems as needed. Cut large mushrooms into 2-inch pieces. Cook mushrooms and garlic in butter in a large Dutch oven over medium-high heat, stirring constantly, until tender. Stir in cheese, pepper, and soy sauce. Garnish, if desired. Yield: 8 servings.

Roasted New Potatoes

2¼	pounds new potatoes, unpeeled and quartered
¼	cup butter or margarine, melted
2	tablespoons vegetable oil
½	teaspoon salt
½	teaspoon dried thyme

Place potato in a 13- x 9- x 2-inch baking dish. Combine butter and remaining ingredients; pour over potato, tossing gently. Bake, uncovered, at 350° for 35 minutes or until tender. Yield: 6 servings.

Potatoes à la Lyonnaise

3	pounds large new potatoes, peeled
¼	cup butter, divided
2	medium onions, thinly sliced and separated into rings
½	teaspoon salt
¼	teaspoon pepper
1	tablespoon chopped fresh parsley

Place potatoes in a Dutch oven; add water to cover. Bring to a boil; cook 8 minutes. Drain; let cool to touch. Cut potatoes into ⅜-inch-thick slices. Melt 2 tablespoons butter in a large skillet. Arrange half of potato slices and half of onion slices in a single layer in skillet; sprinkle with half of salt and pepper. Cook over medium heat, turning frequently, until potato slices are tender and golden. Transfer to a serving dish; keep warm. Repeat procedure with remaining butter, potato, onion, salt, and pepper. Transfer to serving dish, and sprinkle with parsley. Yield: 8 servings.

Mushroom-Shaped Truffled Potatoes

3	large baking potatoes (about 2 pounds)
2	egg yolks
¼	cup finely chopped truffles or wild mushrooms
¼	teaspoon salt
¼	teaspoon ground white pepper
¼	teaspoon ground nutmeg
½	cup all-purpose flour
1	large egg, beaten
1	tablespoon milk
¼	teaspoon salt
¼	teaspoon ground white pepper
1	cup fine, dry breadcrumbs
	Vegetable oil

Cook potatoes in boiling water to cover 40 minutes or until tender; drain and let cool slightly. Peel potatoes, and cut into cubes. Place potato cubes in a large mixing bowl; beat at medium speed of an electric mixer until fluffy. Add 2 egg yolks, one at a time, beating well after each addition. Add truffles and next 3 ingredients; beat well. Cool completely.

Shape mixture into 2-inch balls; sprinkle evenly with flour. Shape one ball into a mushroom, bringing stem upward. Repeat procedure with remaining portions of potato. Combine egg and next 3 ingredients; dip each "mushroom" in egg mixture; gently dredge in breadcrumbs. Pour oil to depth of 6 inches into a Dutch oven; heat to 375°. Fry "mushrooms," in batches, in hot oil 3 minutes or until golden, turning once. Drain on paper towels. Serve immediately. Yield: 20 "mushrooms."

Vegetable Medley

1	small carrot, diagonally sliced
1	teaspoon minced garlic
¼	cup butter or margarine, melted
1	cup cauliflower flowerets
1	cup broccoli flowerets
½	cup julienne-sliced sweet red pepper strips
½	cup julienne-sliced green pepper strips
½	cup julienne-sliced onion
1	small yellow squash, thinly sliced
1	small zucchini, thinly sliced
¼	teaspoon salt
¼	teaspoon ground ginger
⅛	teaspoon ground white pepper

Cook carrot and garlic in butter in a large skillet over medium-high heat, stirring constantly, 3 minutes. Add cauliflower and next 6 ingredients; cook, stirring constantly, 3 minutes or until crisp-tender. Stir in salt, ginger, and pepper. Yield: 4 servings.

Colorful Vegetable Sauté

¼	cup olive oil
¾	teaspoon salt
½	teaspoon ground celery seeds
¼	teaspoon pepper
1	clove garlic, minced
2	large zucchini, cut into very thin strips
2	large carrots, scraped and cut into very thin strips
2	large sweet red peppers, seeded and cut into very thin strips

Combine first 5 ingredients in a large skillet; place over medium heat until hot. Add zucchini, carrot, and red pepper; cook, stirring constantly, 5 to 6 minutes or until tender. Yield: 8 to 10 servings.

Orange-Poached Pears with White Chocolate and Raspberries

4	firm ripe pears with stems
2½	cups orange juice
½	cup dry white wine
½	cup sugar
¼	teaspoon ground cinnamon
8	ounces white chocolate, finely chopped
⅓	cup whipping cream
2	tablespoons seedless raspberry jam
1	teaspoon orange juice
	Fresh raspberries
	Garnish: fresh mint sprigs

Peel pears; core from bottom, cutting to, but not through, the stem end, leaving stems intact.
Combine 2½ cups orange juice and next 3 ingredients in a large saucepan; bring to a boil.
Add pears, standing them upright; cover, reduce heat, and simmer 10 minutes or until pears are tender, basting often with orange juice mixture. Remove from heat; drain pears on paper towels.

Combine chocolate and whipping cream in top of a double boiler; bring water to a boil. Reduce heat to low; cook until chocolate melts, stirring occasionally. Combine jam and 1 teaspoon orange juice in a small saucepan. Cook over low heat, stirring constantly, until jam melts.

Spoon white chocolate sauce evenly onto 4 dessert plates. Place 1 pear upright in center of sauce on each plate. Spoon raspberry mixture evenly in small circles over sauce around each pear. Pull a wooden pick or the tip of a knife continuously through raspberry circles surrounding each pear; arrange raspberries over sauce. Garnish, if desired. Yield: 4 servings.

Compote of Oranges and Coconut

1	cup sugar
2	cups water
1	tablespoon grated orange rind
2	teaspoons grated lemon rind
2	tablespoons lemon juice
5	large oranges, peeled and sectioned
⅔	cup grated coconut
½	cup plus 2 tablespoons whipping cream
¼	cup sifted powdered sugar
2	tablespoons chopped pistachio nuts

Combine first 5 ingredients in a saucepan. Bring to a boil; boil 25 minutes or until thickened, stirring occasionally. Remove from heat; let cool slightly. Layer one-third of orange sections in a 1-quart bowl; sprinkle with one-third of coconut. Drizzle one-third of syrup over coconut. Repeat layers twice. Beat whipping cream until foamy; gradually add powdered sugar, beating until soft peaks form. Top dessert with whipped cream mixture; sprinkle with nuts. Yield: 4 to 6 servings.

Strawberries Zabaglione

2	tablespoons sugar
2	tablespoons Marsala wine, sherry, or port
2	egg yolks
1	cup whipping cream
¼	cup sifted powdered sugar
2½ to 3	dozen large strawberries, washed and capped

Combine first 3 ingredients in top of a double boiler; beat at medium speed of an electric mixer until blended. Place over boiling water. Reduce heat to low, and cook, beating constantly at medium speed, about 5 minutes or until soft peaks form. Transfer mixture to a medium bowl; place bowl in a larger bowl of ice. Beat about 2 minutes or until cool; chill 30 minutes.

Combine whipping cream and powdered sugar; stir well. Cover and chill 30 minutes. Add whipping cream mixture to egg yolk mixture; beat until stiff peaks form.

Cut an **X** in pointed end of each strawberry, cutting to within ½ inch of stem end. Carefully spread apart cut sections of each strawberry to form a cup. Using a pastry bag, pipe whipped cream mixture evenly into each strawberry cup. Chill until ready to serve. Yield: 2½ to 3 dozen.

Raspberry-Fudge Layered Dessert

2	cups vanilla ice cream, slightly softened
½	cup finely chopped toasted pecans
2	cups raspberry sorbet, softened
2	cups chocolate fudge ice cream, softened
	Chocolate Sauce
	Garnishes: fresh raspberries, fresh mint sprigs

Line a greased 9- x 5- x 3-inch loafpan with plastic wrap. Combine vanilla ice cream and pecans, stirring well. Spread in prepared pan. Freeze 30 minutes. Spread sorbet over ice cream layer. Freeze 30 minutes. Spread chocolate ice cream over top. Cover and freeze at least 8 hours.

To unmold, wrap a damp warm towel around loafpan; run a knife or metal spatula around edges to loosen dessert. Invert dessert onto a cutting board; peel off plastic wrap. Cut dessert into ¾-inch slices, using an electric knife. Spoon Chocolate Sauce evenly onto dessert plates; top each serving with a slice of dessert. Garnish, if desired. Serve immediately. Yield: 12 servings.

Chocolate Sauce

1	(12-ounce) package semisweet chocolate morsels
¼	cup butter or margarine
½	cup water
½	cup light corn syrup
¼	cup raspberry schnapps or other raspberry-flavored liqueur

Combine chocolate and butter in top of a double boiler; bring water to a boil. Reduce heat; cook until chocolate melts. Stir in remaining ingredients; let cool. Yield: 2¾ cups.

Praline Ice Cream

2¼ cups sugar
⅓ cup all-purpose flour
½ teaspoon salt
3 large eggs, lightly beaten
5 cups milk
1 quart whipping cream
1½ tablespoons vanilla extract
3½ cups coarsely chopped pralines

Combine first 3 ingredients in a Dutch oven. Add eggs, and stir until smooth. Stir in milk. Cook over medium heat, stirring constantly, until thermometer reaches 160°. Remove from heat, and let cool slightly; cover and chill 2 hours.

Combine whipping cream and vanilla in a large bowl; add chilled custard, stirring with a wire whisk until blended. Pour mixture into freezer can of a 1-gallon hand-turned or electric freezer. Freeze according to manufacturer's instructions. Remove paddle; fold in pralines. Pack freezer with additional ice and rock salt, and let stand 1 hour before serving. Yield: 1 gallon.

Champagne Sorbet

2 cups club soda
1 cup sugar
½ cup orange juice
¼ cup lemon juice
2½ cups champagne
2 tablespoons champagne, divided
    Garnish: sliced fresh strawberries, fresh mint sprigs

Combine first 4 ingredients in a medium saucepan; bring to a boil. Reduce heat to medium, and cook, stirring constantly, until sugar dissolves. Cover and chill thoroughly.

Gently stir 2½ cups champagne into chilled mixture; pour into freezer container of a 2-quart hand-turned or electric freezer. Freeze according to manufacturer's instructions. Pack freezer with additional ice and rock salt, and let stand 1 hour before serving.

Scoop sorbet into individual dessert bowls; top each serving with 1 teaspoon champagne. Garnish, if desired. Yield: 6 servings.

Chocolate Fudge Cake

⅓   cup water
2   (1-ounce) squares unsweetened chocolate
⅔   cup shortening
2¾   cups sugar, divided
2   large eggs
2½   cups all-purpose flour
1¾   teaspoons baking soda
¾   teaspoon salt, divided
1   cup buttermilk
1   tablespoon plus 1 teaspoon vanilla extract, divided
¼   cup all-purpose flour
1   cup milk
½   cup butter, softened
½   cup shortening
    Chocolate Frosting

Combine water and chocolate in a small heavy saucepan; cook over low heat, stirring constantly, until chocolate melts. Remove from heat; let cool.

Beat ⅔ cup shortening at medium speed of an electric mixer until creamy; gradually add 1¾ cups sugar, beating well. Add eggs, one at a time; beat well after each addition. Combine 2½ cups flour, soda, and ½ teaspoon salt; add to shortening mixture alternately with buttermilk, beginning and ending with flour mixture. Mix after each addition. Add cooled chocolate mixture and 1 teaspoon vanilla; mix just until blended.

Pour batter into 3 greased and floured 9-inch round cakepans. Bake at 350° for 17 to 19 minutes or until a wooden pick inserted in center comes out clean. Cool in pans on wire racks 10 minutes; remove from pans, and let cool completely on wire racks.

Place ¼ cup flour in a small saucepan; gradually stir in milk. Cook over low heat, stirring constantly, until thick. Remove from heat; let cool completely.

Beat butter and ½ cup shortening at medium speed until creamy; gradually add remaining 1 cup sugar, beating well. Add remaining 1 tablespoon vanilla, remaining ¼ teaspoon salt, and flour mixture; beat until smooth. Spread filling between cake layers. Spread Chocolate Frosting on top and sides of cake. Yield: one 3-layer cake.

Chocolate Frosting

3   cups sugar
¾   cup milk
¾   cup butter or margarine
3   (1-ounce) squares unsweetened chocolate
¾   teaspoon vanilla extract

Combine first 4 ingredients in a saucepan; cook over low heat, stirring constantly, until chocolate melts. Cook over medium heat, stirring constantly, until mixture boils; boil 1 minute, stirring constantly. Remove from heat; stir in vanilla. Beat at high speed of an electric mixer until frosting is spreading consistency. Immediately spread on cake. Yield: enough for one 3-layer cake.

Gold Cake

½ cup butter or margarine, softened
1¾ cups sugar
4 egg yolks
1 large egg
2½ cups sifted cake flour
1 tablespoon baking powder
½ teaspoon salt
½ teaspoon ground mace
1 cup plus 3 tablespoons milk
Lemon Fluff Frosting

Beat butter at medium speed of an electric mixer until creamy; gradually add sugar, beating well. Add egg yolks and egg, one at a time, beating after each addition.

Combine flour and next 3 ingredients; add to butter mixture alternately with milk, beginning and ending with flour mixture. Mix after each addition.

Pour batter into a greased and floured 10-inch tube pan. Bake at 350° for 60 to 65 minutes or until a wooden pick inserted in center comes out clean. Cool in pan on a wire rack 10 minutes; remove from pan, and let cool completely on wire rack. Spread Lemon Fluff Frosting on top and sides of cake. Yield: one 10-inch cake.

Lemon Fluff Frosting

¾ cup butter or margarine, softened
6 cups sifted powdered sugar
1 tablespoon grated lemon rind
3 to 4 tablespoons lemon juice

Beat butter at medium speed of an electric mixer until creamy; gradually add powdered sugar, beating until mixture is light and fluffy. Add lemon rind and juice; beat until mixture is smooth. Yield: 3 cups.

Coconut-Cream Cheese Pound Cake

1 (8-ounce) package cream cheese, softened
½ cup butter or margarine, softened
½ cup shortening
3 cups sugar
6 large eggs
3 cups all-purpose flour
¼ teaspoon baking soda
¼ teaspoon salt
2 cups flaked coconut
1 teaspoon vanilla extract
1 teaspoon coconut extract

Beat cream cheese, butter, and shortening at medium speed of an electric mixer about 2 minutes or until soft and creamy. Gradually add sugar, beating at medium speed 5 to 7 minutes. Add eggs, one at a time, beating just until yellow disappears.

Combine flour, soda, and salt; add to butter mixture, mixing just until blended. Stir in coconut and flavorings. Pour batter into a greased and floured 10-inch tube pan. Bake at 350° for 1 hour and 20 minutes or until a wooden pick inserted in center comes out clean. Cool in pan on a wire rack 10 to 15 minutes; remove from pan, and let cool completely on wire rack. Yield: one 10-inch cake.

Pumpkin Roll

¾	cup all-purpose flour
1	teaspoon baking powder
½	teaspoon salt
2	teaspoons ground cinnamon
1	teaspoon ground nutmeg
1	teaspoon ground ginger
4	large eggs
1	cup sugar
⅔	cup canned pumpkin
1	teaspoon lemon juice
1 to 2	tablespoons sifted powdered sugar
1	(8-ounce) package cream cheese, softened
¼	cup butter, softened
1¾	cups sifted powdered sugar
1	teaspoon vanilla extract
1	cup chopped walnuts
	Additional powdered sugar (optional)

Combine first 6 ingredients; set aside.

Beat eggs in a mixing bowl at high speed of an electric mixer until thick; gradually add 1 cup sugar, beating 5 minutes. Stir in pumpkin and lemon juice. Gradually stir flour mixture into pumpkin mixture. Spread batter in a greased and floured 15- x 10- x 1-inch jellyroll pan. Bake at 375° for 12 to 15 minutes or until a wooden pick inserted in center comes out clean.

Sift 1 to 2 tablespoons powdered sugar in a 15- x 10-inch rectangle on a cloth towel. When cake is done, immediately loosen from sides of pan, and turn out onto sugared towel. Starting at narrow end, roll up cake and towel together; cool completely on a wire rack, seam side down.

Beat cream cheese and butter in a large bowl at high speed until creamy; gradually add 1¾ cups powdered sugar and vanilla, beating well. Stir in walnuts.

Unroll cake, and remove towel. Spread cake evenly with cream cheese mixture; carefully reroll cake. Place cake roll, seam side down, on a serving platter. Cover and chill until filling is firm. Sprinkle with powdered sugar, if desired. Yield: 10 servings.

Petits Fours

         1   cup shortening
         2   cups sugar
         3   cups all-purpose flour
         2   teaspoons baking powder
        ¼   teaspoon salt
         1   cup ice water
        1½   teaspoons imitation butter flavor
         1   teaspoon vanilla or ½ teaspoon almond extract
         4   egg whites
        ½   teaspoon cream of tartar
        10   cups sifted powdered sugar
         1   cup water
         3   tablespoons light corn syrup
         1   teaspoon vanilla or almond extract
               Creamy Decorator Frosting

Beat shortening at medium speed of an electric mixer until creamy; gradually add 2 cups sugar, beating well. Combine flour, baking powder, and salt; add to creamed mixture alternately with ice water, beginning and ending with flour mixture. Mix after each addition. Stir in flavorings.

Beat egg whites and cream of tartar at high speed until soft peaks form. Gently fold one-third of beaten egg white into batter; fold in remaining beaten egg white. Pour batter into 2 greased and floured 8-inch square pans. Bake at 325° for 40 to 45 minutes. Cool in pans on wire racks 10 minutes; remove from pans, and let cool completely on wire racks. Cover; freeze until firm.

Trim crusts from all surfaces, making sure tops of cakes are flat. Cut each cake into 16 (2-inch) squares; brush away loose crumbs. Place squares 2 inches apart on wire racks in a jellyroll pan.

Combine powdered sugar and next 3 ingredients in a saucepan; cook over low heat, stirring constantly, until mixture reaches 110°. Quickly pour warm icing over cake squares, completely covering tops and sides. Spoon up all excess icing; reheat to 110°. (If necessary, add a small amount of water to maintain icing's original consistency.) Continue pouring and reheating icing until all cakes have been iced twice. Let icing dry completely. Trim any excess icing from bottom of each cake square. Decorate as desired with Creamy Decorator Frosting. Yield: 32 petits fours.

Creamy Decorator Frosting
         2   cups sifted powdered sugar
        ¼   cup plus 2 tablespoons shortening
         2   tablespoons milk
        ½   teaspoon vanilla or almond extract
               Dash of salt
               Paste food coloring

Combine first 5 ingredients in a small mixing bowl; beat at low speed of an electric mixer until smooth. Color frosting in small amounts with desired paste food coloring. (Keep frosting covered with a damp cloth or plastic wrap.) Yield: 1¼ cups.

Marjolaine

1	egg white
¾	cup almond paste
6	large eggs, separated
½	cup sugar
½	teaspoon vanilla extract
¼	cup sugar
½	cup plus 2 tablespoons sifted cake flour
½	cup plus 2 tablespoons cocoa, divided
1½	cups slivered almonds, toasted
1	cup hazelnuts, toasted and skinned
1	tablespoon bread flour
8	egg whites
1¼	cups sugar
1	tablespoon powdered sugar
	Ganache
	Praline Buttercream
	Garnishes: sliced kiwifruit, sliced strawberries

Combine 1 egg white and almond paste; beat at medium speed of an electric mixer until blended. Beat egg yolks and ½ cup sugar at medium speed 6 minutes or until mixture is very thick and falls from the beater in a long, flat stream that folds upon itself. Stir in vanilla. Slowly add yolk mixture to almond mixture, stirring constantly. (Lumps will form if added too fast.)

Beat 6 egg whites at high speed of electric mixer until foamy. Gradually add ¼ cup sugar, 1 tablespoon at a time, beating until stiff peaks form and sugar dissolves (2 to 4 minutes). Fold egg white mixture into yolk mixture.

Sift together cake flour and ½ cup plus 1 tablespoon cocoa; fold into egg mixture. Spoon into an 18- x 12- x 1-inch jellyroll pan lined with wax paper, spreading evenly. Bake at 350° for 12 minutes or until a wooden pick inserted in center comes out clean.

Sift 1 tablespoon cocoa in an 18- x 12-inch rectangle on a towel. When cake is done, immediately loosen from pan, and turn out onto towel. Peel off wax paper. Cool; cut in half crosswise.

Position knife blade in food processor bowl; add almonds and hazelnuts. Process until nuts are finely ground. Stir bread flour into nuts.

Beat 8 egg whites at high speed of an electric mixer until foamy. Gradually add 1¼ cups sugar, 1 tablespoon at a time, beating until stiff peaks form and sugar dissolves (2 to 4 minutes). Gently fold one-third of egg white mixture into nut mixture; fold in remaining egg white mixture. Spoon batter into same jellyroll pan again lined with wax paper. Bake at 350° for 15 to 20 minutes or until lightly browned.

Sift powdered sugar in an 18- x 12-inch rectangle on a towel. Turn meringue out onto a towel; remove wax paper, and let cool completely. Cut meringue in half crosswise.

Place one layer of cake on a cake plate; spread 3 tablespoons Ganache over cake, and top with 1 layer of meringue. Spread Praline Buttercream over meringue. Place remaining layer of cake over buttercream; spread 3 tablespoons Ganache over cake, and top with remaining meringue layer. Frost top and sides of cake with remaining Ganache. Cover and chill 2 to 24 hours. Garnish, if desired. Yield: 12 servings.

Ganache

  1⅓   cups whipping cream
   2   egg yolks
   ¼   cup sugar
   ½   teaspoon vanilla extract
  3½   (4-ounce) packages sweet dark baking chocolate, broken into small pieces

Combine first 4 ingredients in a medium saucepan; cook over low heat, stirring constantly, until mixture is 160°. Remove from heat; add chocolate, stirring until melted. Let cool. Yield: 2½ cups.

Praline Buttercream

   ½   cup hazelnuts, toasted and skinned
  2⅔   cups plus 2½ teaspoons sifted powdered sugar, divided
   1   cup butter or margarine, softened
   1   tablespoon milk
   ½   teaspoon vanilla extract

Position knife blade in food processor bowl; add nuts and 2½ teaspoons powdered sugar. Process until mixture is like a paste.
Beat butter at medium speed of an electric mixer until creamy; gradually add remaining 2⅔ cups powdered sugar, beating until light and fluffy. Add milk; beat until spreading consistency. Stir in vanilla. Stir in hazelnut paste. Yield: 2½ cups.

Mint Chocolate Cheesecake

          Vegetable cooking spray
   ¾   cup chocolate wafer crumbs
   6   (8-ounce) packages cream cheese, softened
   3   cups sugar
  12   large eggs
  1¼   cups chopped chocolate-covered mint wafer candies (about 34 candies), divided

Coat a 10-inch springform pan with cooking spray. Sprinkle chocolate wafer crumbs evenly over bottom of pan. Set aside.
Beat cream cheese at medium speed of a heavy-duty electric mixer until creamy; gradually add sugar, beating well. Add eggs, one at a time, beating after each addition. Stir in 1 cup chopped candies. Pour mixture into prepared crust; sprinkle evenly with remaining chopped candies. Place pan in a large shallow pan. Add hot water to larger pan to depth of 2 inches. Bake on lowest rack of oven at 350° for 1 hour and 30 minutes. Turn oven off, and leave cheesecake in closed oven 1 hour. Remove cheesecake from water bath; let cool in springform pan on a wire rack. Cover and chill. Carefully remove sides of springform pan. Yield: one 10-inch cheesecake.

Orange Cheesecake with Raspberry Sauce

Vegetable cooking spray
¼ cup graham cracker crumbs
6 (8-ounce) packages cream cheese, softened
3 cups sugar
12 large eggs
3½ tablespoons grated orange rind
⅓ cup fresh orange juice
Raspberry Sauce

Coat a 10-inch springform pan with cooking spray. Sprinkle graham cracker crumbs evenly over bottom and up sides of pan. Set aside.

Beat cream cheese at medium speed of a heavy-duty electric mixer until fluffy. Gradually add sugar; beat well. Add eggs, two at a time; beat after each addition. Stir in orange rind and juice. Pour into prepared crust; place pan in a large shallow pan. Add hot water to depth of 1 inch to larger pan. Bake on lowest rack of oven at 350° for 1 hour and 30 minutes. Turn off oven; leave in closed oven 1 hour. Remove cheesecake from water bath; let cool to room temperature in pan on a wire rack. Chill at least 8 hours. Remove sides of springform pan. Serve with Raspberry Sauce. Yield: 16 servings.

Raspberry Sauce

4 cups fresh or frozen unsweetened raspberries, thawed
½ cup sugar
¼ cup orange juice

Combine all ingredients in a saucepan; bring to a boil. Reduce heat, and simmer 10 minutes, stirring occasionally. Place mixture in a strainer; press raspberries against sides of strainer to squeeze out juice. Discard pulp and seeds remaining in strainer. Yield: 1¼ cups.

Rum Pecan Pie

1 cup sugar
1 cup light corn syrup
½ cup butter or margarine, melted
3 tablespoons rum
1 teaspoon vanilla extract
¼ teaspoon salt
4 large eggs, lightly beaten
1 unbaked 9-inch pastry shell
1 to 1¼ cups pecan halves

Combine first 3 ingredients in a small saucepan; cook over low heat, stirring constantly, until sugar dissolves. Remove from heat; let cool slightly. Stir in rum and next 3 ingredients.

Pour filling into pastry shell, and top with pecan halves. Bake at 325° for 50 to 55 minutes. Serve warm or chilled. Yield: one 9-inch pie.

Lemon Meringue Pie

1   cup sugar
3   tablespoons cornstarch
¼   teaspoon salt
2   cups milk
4   large eggs, separated
1   teaspoon grated lemon rind
⅓   cup fresh lemon juice
3   tablespoons butter or margarine
1   baked 9-inch pastry shell
½   teaspoon cream of tartar
¼   cup plus 2 tablespoons sugar
½   teaspoon vanilla extract

Combine 1 cup sugar, cornstarch, and salt in a heavy saucepan. Gradually add milk, stirring until blended. Cook over medium heat, stirring constantly, until mixture thickens and comes to a boil. Boil 1 minute, stirring constantly. Remove from heat.

Beat egg yolks at high speed of an electric mixer until thick and pale. Gradually stir about one-fourth of hot mixture into yolks; add to remaining hot mixture, stirring constantly. Cook over medium heat, stirring constantly, 3 minutes. Remove from heat; add lemon rind, lemon juice, and butter, stirring until butter melts. Spoon mixture into pastry shell.

Beat egg whites and cream of tartar at high speed 1 minute. Gradually add ¼ cup plus 2 table-spoons sugar, 1 tablespoon at a time, beating until stiff peaks form and sugar dissolves (2 to 4 minutes). Add vanilla; beat well. Spread meringue evenly over hot filling, sealing to edge of pastry. Bake at 325° for 25 minutes or until golden. Yield: one 9-inch pie.

Peach Cobbler

3⅓ cups all-purpose flour, divided
1½ teaspoons salt
¾ teaspoon baking powder
¾ cup shortening
½ to ⅔ cup cold water
8 cups peeled, sliced fresh peaches
2 cups sugar
¾ cup water
½ cup butter or margarine, melted
1 teaspoon ground cinnamon
1 teaspoon almond extract

Combine 3 cups flour, salt, and baking powder; cut in shortening until mixture is crumbly. Sprinkle enough cold water (1 tablespoon at a time) over surface to moisten dry ingredients, stirring with a fork after each addition. Shape into a ball. Set pastry aside.

Combine peaches and ⅓ cup flour; toss gently to coat peaches. Stir in sugar and remaining ingredients. Roll two-thirds of pastry to a 15- x 11-inch rectangle on a floured surface; place in a lightly greased 13- x 9- x 2-inch baking dish. Spoon peach mixture over pastry in dish. Roll remaining pastry to ¼-inch thickness; cut into ½-inch strips. Arrange strips in a lattice design over peach mixture. Bake at 350° for 1 hour and 15 minutes or until pastry is golden. Yield: 8 to 10 servings.

North Carolina Apple and Hazelnut Tart

1 cup plus 1 tablespoon all-purpose flour, divided
⅓ cup sugar
½ cup chopped hazelnuts, divided
¼ teaspoon vanilla extract
½ cup butter
1 (8-ounce) package cream cheese, softened
¼ cup sugar
1 large egg, lightly beaten
1 tablespoon Frangelico or other hazelnut-flavored liqueur
1 tablespoon sugar
½ teaspoon ground cinnamon
2 small cooking apples, peeled and thinly sliced

Combine 1 cup flour, ⅓ cup sugar, ¼ cup hazelnuts, and vanilla; cut in butter until mixture is crumbly. Press mixture into bottom and up sides of a 9-inch tart pan. Bake at 350° for 15 minutes. Beat cream cheese and ¼ cup sugar at medium speed of an electric mixer until creamy. Add egg and liqueur; beat well. Pour into crust. Combine remaining 1 tablespoon flour, 1 tablespoon sugar, and cinnamon; sprinkle over apple slices, and toss gently. Overlap slices in a circle over cream cheese mixture; sprinkle with remaining ¼ cup hazelnuts. Bake at 350° for 50 minutes or until cheese mixture is set. Yield: one 9-inch tart.

Peach Cobbler, Caramel Fudge (page 149)

Apple Turnovers

2	small cooking apples, peeled and thinly sliced
½	cup sifted powdered sugar
1	tablespoon butter
1	tablespoon water
½	teaspoon grated lemon rind
⅛	teaspoon ground cinnamon
	Pastry
¼	cup apricot preserves
1	large egg, lightly beaten
	Sugar

Combine first 6 ingredients in a medium saucepan; cover and cook over medium heat until apple is almost tender, stirring often. Remove from heat, and set aside.

Roll pastry to ⅛-inch thickness on a lightly floured surface; cut into rounds with a 4½-inch round cutter. Place 2 tablespoons apple mixture in center of each pastry round; top each with 1 teaspoon preserves. Moisten edges of pastry rounds with water; fold pastry over apple mixture, and crimp edges. Place turnovers on greased baking sheets; brush with egg, and sprinkle with sugar. Bake at 425° for 12 minutes or until lightly browned. Yield: 1 dozen.

Pastry

2	cups all-purpose flour
¾	teaspoon salt
⅓	cup shortening, chilled
¼	cup butter, chilled
3	tablespoons cold water

Combine flour and salt; cut in shortening and butter with pastry blender until mixture is crumbly. Sprinkle cold water (1 tablespoon at a time) evenly over surface; stir with a fork until dry ingredients are moistened. Shape into a ball; chill 1 hour. Yield: enough pastry for 1 dozen turnovers.

Apple Walnut Crêpes

½ cup sifted cake flour
¼ cup plus 2 tablespoons bread flour
2 tablespoons sugar
½ teaspoon salt
2 large eggs, lightly beaten
1 egg yolk, lightly beaten
¾ cup warm milk (105° to 115°)
4½ tablespoons butter, melted and divided
1 tablespoon brandy
Vegetable oil
3 Granny Smith apples, peeled and chopped
⅓ cup firmly packed brown sugar
½ cup chopped walnuts
1½ teaspoons ground cinnamon
½ teaspoon ground allspice
¼ teaspoon ground nutmeg
1 (8-ounce) package cream cheese, softened
¼ cup honey
Caramel Sauce
Garnish: whipped cream

Combine first 4 ingredients; stir well. Add eggs and egg yolk, stirring just until dry ingredients are moistened. Gradually add milk, 3 tablespoons melted butter, and brandy, beating at medium speed of an electric mixer until smooth. Let batter stand at room temperature 1 hour.

Brush bottom of a 6-inch crêpe pan or heavy skillet with oil; place over medium heat until just hot, not smoking. Pour 2 tablespoons batter into pan; quickly tilt pan in all directions so batter covers pan in a thin film. Cook 1 minute or until crêpe can be shaken loose from pan. Flip crêpe, and cook about 30 seconds. Place crêpes on a towel to cool. Stack between layers of wax paper to prevent sticking. Repeat until all batter is used, making 14 crêpes.

Place remaining 1½ tablespoons melted butter in a large skillet over medium-high heat. Add apple and brown sugar; cook 4 minutes, stirring constantly. Stir in walnuts and next 3 ingredients; cook an additional 2 minutes, stirring constantly. Remove from heat, and let cool completely.

Beat cream cheese at medium speed until creamy; gradually add honey, beating well. Stir in apple mixture. Spoon about 3 tablespoons apple mixture in center of each crêpe; roll up. To serve, place 2 filled crêpes, seam side down, on each dessert plate; top with Caramel Sauce. Garnish, if desired. Yield: 7 servings.

Caramel Sauce

1¾ cups firmly packed brown sugar
½ cup butter
½ cup half-and-half

Combine brown sugar and butter in a saucepan; cook over medium heat, stirring constantly, until sugar dissolves and butter melts. Stir in half-and-half. Serve warm. Yield: about 2 cups.

Banana Pudding

1⅓ cups sugar
3½ tablespoons all-purpose flour
    Dash of salt
3 large eggs, separated
3 cups milk
1 teaspoon vanilla extract
1 (12-ounce) package vanilla wafers
6 medium bananas
¼ cup plus 2 tablespoons sugar
1 teaspoon vanilla extract

Combine first 3 ingredients in a heavy saucepan. Beat egg yolks until thick; add milk, and mix well. Add to dry ingredients, stirring well. Cook over medium heat, stirring constantly, until smooth and thickened. Remove from heat; stir in 1 teaspoon vanilla.

Arrange one-third of wafers in the bottom of a 3-quart baking dish. Slice 2 bananas, and layer over wafers. Pour one-third of pudding mixture over bananas. Repeat layers twice.

Beat egg whites at high speed of an electric mixer until foamy. Gradually add ¼ cup plus 2 tablespoons sugar, 1 tablespoon at a time, beating until stiff peaks form. Add 1 teaspoon vanilla, and beat until blended. Spread meringue evenly over pudding, sealing to edge of dish. Bake at 325° for 25 to 28 minutes or until meringue is golden. Yield: 8 to 10 servings.

Bird's Nest Pudding

8 large cooking apples, unpeeled and cored
1 cup plus 2 tablespoons sugar, divided
¼ cup plus 3 tablespoons all-purpose flour
4 cups milk
3 large eggs, lightly beaten
1 large egg, separated
1½ teaspoons vanilla extract
1½ teaspoons sugar

Place apples in a 13- x 9- x 2-inch baking dish; fill apple centers evenly with ½ cup sugar. Add water to dish to depth of ½ inch. Bake, uncovered, at 350° for 40 minutes or until apples are tender. Drain apples on paper towels; discard liquid. Return apples to dish; set aside.

Combine ½ cup plus 2 tablespoons sugar and flour in top of a double boiler. Gradually add milk; stir well. Combine 3 eggs and egg yolk; add to milk mixture, stirring with a wire whisk. Bring water to a boil. Reduce heat to medium; cook, stirring constantly, 18 to 20 minutes or until mixture thickens and coats a metal spoon. Stir in vanilla. Pour custard around apples.

Beat egg white at high speed of an electric mixer until foamy; add 1½ teaspoons sugar, beating until stiff peaks form. Dollop meringue evenly on top of each apple. Bake at 325° for 12 minutes or until meringue is golden. Spoon a baked apple and custard into each individual serving bowl. Serve immediately. Yield: 8 servings.

Bread Pudding

1   (1-pound) loaf French bread
1   quart milk
3   large eggs, lightly beaten
1½ cups sugar
1   cup raisins
2   tablespoons vanilla extract
3   tablespoons butter or margarine, melted
    Whiskey Sauce

Break bread into small chunks, and place in a large bowl. Add milk; stir well. Let stand 15 minutes. Combine eggs and next 3 ingredients; add to bread mixture, stirring well. Pour butter into a 13- x 9- x 2-inch pan; spoon bread mixture into pan. Bake at 350° for 25 minutes or until set. Cool; cut into squares. Place pudding in dessert dishes, and spoon Whiskey Sauce over top of each serving. Yield: 12 to 15 servings.

Whiskey Sauce
1   cup sugar
½   cup butter
½   cup half-and-half
2   tablespoons whiskey

Combine first 3 ingredients in a heavy saucepan. Bring to a boil over medium heat; reduce heat, and simmer 5 minutes. Remove from heat; let cool. Stir in whiskey. Yield: 1½ cups.

Hasty Pudding

2   tablespoons butter or margarine
3   tablespoons all-purpose flour
1½ cups milk
1   large egg, lightly beaten
1½ tablespoons brown sugar
    Dash of ground cinnamon
    Dash of freshly grated nutmeg
1   tablespoon butter or margarine

Melt 2 tablespoons butter in a saucepan over low heat. Add flour; stir until smooth. Cook 1 minute, stirring constantly. Gradually add milk; cook over medium heat, stirring constantly, until mixture thickens. Gradually stir about one-fourth of hot mixture into egg; add to remaining hot mixture, stirring constantly. Cook, stirring constantly, until thickened.

Pour mixture into a greased 1-quart casserole. Combine brown sugar, cinnamon, and nutmeg; sprinkle over pudding mixture. Dot evenly with 1 tablespoon butter. Broil 5½ inches from heat (with electric oven door partially opened) 4 minutes or until butter melts and pudding is lightly browned. Yield: 4 servings.

Plum Pudding

½   cup butter, softened
1   cup sugar
6   large eggs
2   cups soft breadcrumbs
2   teaspoons ground cinnamon
½   teaspoon ground cloves
½   teaspoon ground allspice
1   cup raisins
1   cup currants
1   cup chopped pecans
2   tablespoons all-purpose flour
    Hot Wine Sauce

Beat butter at medium speed of an electric mixer until creamy; gradually add sugar, beating well. Add eggs, one at a time; beat after each addition. Combine breadcrumbs and next 3 ingredients; stir well. Combine raisins and next three ingredients; stir well. Add breadcrumb mixture and raisin mixture to butter mixture, stirring well. Spoon into a greased 11- x 7- x 1½-inch baking dish. Bake at 375° for 30 minutes or until set. Serve with Hot Wine Sauce. Yield: 8 servings.

Hot Wine Sauce
2   cups dry white wine
2   cups orange juice
1   cup sugar

Combine ingredients in a saucepan. Cook and stir until sugar dissolves. Yield: 5 cups.

Tiramisù

1¼   cups sugar
6   egg yolks
1¼   cups mascarpone cheese*
1¾   cups whipping cream
¾   cup water
1½   tablespoons brandy
2   teaspoons instant coffee granules
2   (3-ounce) packages ladyfingers, split lengthwise
     Garnishes: piped whipped cream, grated unsweetened chocolate

Combine sugar and egg yolks in top of a double boiler; beat at medium speed of an electric mixer until thick and pale. Bring water to a boil; reduce heat to low, and cook, stirring constantly, 8 to 10 minutes. Remove from heat; add mascarpone cheese, and beat until smooth.
Beat whipping cream at high speed until soft peaks form; fold into cheese mixture. Combine water, brandy, and coffee granules; brush mixture onto cut sides of ladyfingers. Line bottom and

sides of a trifle bowl or 3-quart soufflé dish with 36 ladyfingers; pour in half of filling. Cover with remaining ladyfingers; top with remaining filling. Cover and chill. Garnish, if desired. Yield: 10 to 12 servings.

*As a substitute for mascarpone cheese, combine 2 (8-ounce) packages cream cheese, softened; ⅓ cup sour cream; and ¼ cup whipping cream, beating well. Use 1¼ cups mixture for recipe, reserving remainder for another use.

Blonde Brownies with Chocolate Chunks

1	(6-ounce) vanilla-flavored baking bar
⅓	cup butter or margarine
2	large eggs, lightly beaten
½	cup sugar
¼	teaspoon vanilla extract
1½	cups all-purpose flour
½	teaspoon baking powder
¼	teaspoon salt
⅔	cup chopped pecans
⅔	cup semisweet chocolate chunks

Combine baking bar and butter in a heavy saucepan; cook over low heat, stirring constantly, until melted. Set aside to cool slightly. Combine eggs, sugar, and vanilla in a large bowl, stirring until blended. Add butter mixture; stir well. Combine flour, baking powder, and salt; stir into butter mixture. Stir in pecans and chocolate chunks. Spoon into a greased 9-inch square pan. Bake at 350° for 25 minutes. Cool on a wire rack; cut into 1½-inch squares. Yield: 3 dozen.

Madeleines

2	large eggs
⅛	teaspoon salt
⅓	cup sugar
¼	teaspoon vanilla extract
½	cup plus 1 tablespoon sifted cake flour
1	teaspoon grated orange rind
½	cup butter, melted and cooled
	Sifted powdered sugar

Beat eggs and salt at high speed of electric mixer until foamy. Gradually add ⅓ cup sugar, beating 5 minutes at high speed or until mixture is light and fluffy. Stir in vanilla.

Combine flour and orange rind; fold into egg mixture, 2 tablespoons at a time. Fold in butter, 1 tablespoon at a time. Spoon 2 tablespoons batter into each greased and floured madeleine mold. Bake at 350° for 12 minutes or until lightly browned. Cool 3 minutes. Remove from molds; cool on a wire rack, flat side down. Sprinkle with powdered sugar. Yield: 1 dozen.

Nutty Apricot Bars

2   (6-ounce) packages dried apricots
¾   cup sugar
¾   cup butter or margarine, softened
1   cup sugar
2   cups all-purpose flour
½   teaspoon baking soda
¼   teaspoon salt
1   (3-ounce) can flaked coconut
½   cup chopped pecans or walnuts

Place apricots in a medium saucepan; add water to cover. Bring to a boil; reduce heat, and simmer, uncovered, 15 minutes or until tender. Drain, reserving ¼ cup liquid. Coarsely chop apricots, and set aside. Combine reserved apricot liquid and ¾ cup sugar in pan; simmer, uncovered, 5 minutes. Stir in chopped apricots; set aside.

Beat butter at medium speed of an electric mixer until creamy; gradually add 1 cup sugar, beating well. Combine flour, soda, and salt; add to butter mixture, mixing well (mixture will be crumbly). Stir in coconut and pecans. Pat about three-fourths of coconut mixture into an ungreased 13- x 9- x 2-inch pan. Bake at 350° for 10 minutes.

Spread apricot mixture evenly over crust, spreading to within ¼ inch from edge of pan. Sprinkle evenly with remaining coconut mixture. Bake for 30 minutes. Cool in pan on a wire rack; cover and chill. Cut into bars. Store in refrigerator. Yield: about 4 dozen.

Hermits

2½   cups all-purpose flour
1   teaspoon baking soda
½   teaspoon salt
1   teaspoon ground nutmeg
1   teaspoon ground cinnamon
1   teaspoon ground cloves
1½   cups sugar
1   cup raisins
½   cup chopped pecans
½   cup vegetable oil
¼   cup milk
3   large eggs, lightly beaten
1   teaspoon vanilla extract

Combine first 6 ingredients in a large mixing bowl. Stir in sugar, raisins, and pecans. Add oil and remaining ingredients, stirring until moistened.

Drop dough by rounded teaspoonfuls 1 inch apart onto lightly greased cookie sheets. Bake at 350° for 8 to 10 minutes or until done. Cool slightly on cookie sheets; remove to wire racks, and let cool completely. Yield: 7 dozen.

Stately Fold

A. Lay napkin open and flat. Fold napkin in half to form a triangle with points facing down towards you.

B. Fold right point down to bottom point; fold left point down to bottom point.

C. Holding points with your left hand, turn napkin over. Then turn napkin so that open points are at top. Then bring bottom point up to meet top point, forming a triangle.

D. Lift up at center of bottom, and allow napkin to stand up.

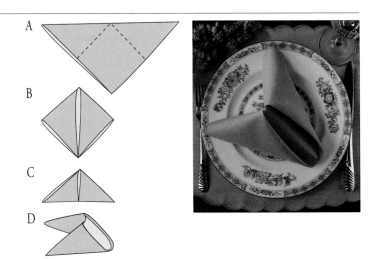

Italian Cap

A. Lay napkin open and flat, wrong side up. Fold four corners together so that points meet in center. Fold four corners to center again.

B. Fold napkin in half widthwise, keeping the triangular folds on the outside. Tuck the top corner points (1 and 2) inside the outer layers to meet at center point (3).

C. Slide right outer folds of triangle into left outer folds until secure.

D. Turn napkin over, and repeat with remaining triangle.

E. Place hand inside napkin, and gently shape cap.

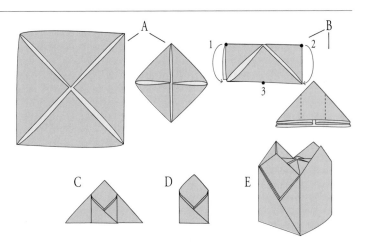

Starburst Fold

A. Lay napkin open and flat, wrong side up. Fold four corners in sharply so that points meet in center.

B. Fold four new corners in so that they also meet in center. Holding folds in place with your left hand, flip napkin over. Then again fold in new corners to meet in center.

C. Hold napkin corners firmly together in center with your left hand. With your right hand, reach underneath each corner and pick up loose point. Sharply pull each loose point outward. Repeat procedure for each corner and point.

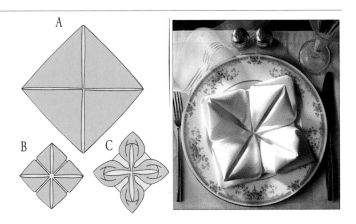

Pairing Food & Wine

Serving wine adds festivity and pleasure to any occasion, and requires no more formality than serving coffee or tea. While there are acknowledged customs regarding the pairing of food and wine, there is no mysterious ritual. Use the following suggestions that are in keeping with the Vanderbilt food and wine philosophy to make serving wine easy and pleasurable.

Pairing wines and foods is more art than science, but an art within the reach of everybody. You can follow some traditional guidelines—such as serving white wines with white meats, red wines with red meat—although you may find it more enjoyable to experiment on your own.

Here are a few tips to get you started:

♦ Sweet foods should generally be paired with sweet wines, but the food should never be sweeter than the wine.

♦ The way you prepare the food is more important in determining the wine than the food itself. For instance, try a light white wine with grilled chicken, but a full-bodied white wine with chicken in cream sauce—and consider a rosé or red wine for chicken in Italian or Chinese cooking.

♦ Try matching or contrasting the flavor and texture of wine with food. For example, match a hearty beef stew with a hearty red wine, or contrast a salty cheese with a sweet wine.

♦ Acidic foods such as tomatoes, citrus fruits, and vinegar pair well with high-acid wines, such as Sauvignon Blanc.

♦ Try serving spicy, salty, or smoked dishes with light, fruity wines, such as Johannisberg Riesling or White Zinfandels.

♦ If serving more than one wine with a meal, serve dry before sweet, white before red, light before full, young before old.

♦ Serving temperature for white and rosé wines should be between 44 and 53 degrees; champagnes, between 39 and 44 degrees; and red wines, between 59 and 68 degrees.

Pairing Cheese & Wine

CHEESE	WINE
Asiago	Full-bodied reds
Brie	Most reds; medium sweet whites; sparkling wines; cream sherries
Camembert	Most reds and whites
Cheddar, mild	Most whites or rosés
Cheddar, sharp	Full-bodied reds
Chévre	Full-bodied reds
Havarti, cream	Sweeter whites and rosés
Havarti, Danish	Dry reds or whites
Feta	Light reds; medium sweet whites
Fontina	Dry reds; for milder versions, most whites
Gouda	Most whites or reds; sherries; ports
Jarlsberg	Most wines
Monterey Jack	Most wines
Mozzarella	Dry reds or whites
Muenster	Light red; rosés; dry whites
Parmesan	Dry reds or whites
Roquefort	Red wines
Stilton	Ports
Swiss	Most reds and whites

Biltmore Estate Wine · Taste & Aroma · Food

Biltmore Estate Wine	Taste & Aroma	Food
WHITE WINES		
Chateau Biltmore Chardonnay Barrel Fermented	Crisp with pear and apple aroma plus soft honey vanilla-oak flavors and a graceful finish	Fish, poultry, vegetables with white sauce
Biltmore Estate Sauvignon Blanc	Tangy and lively with great herbal varietal flavors with nuances of peach	Fish, shrimp, shellfish
Biltmore Estate Chardonnay sur Lies	Grapefruit and pineapple aroma with buttery nuances; crisp and medium bodied	Oysters, grilled seafood, veal, poultry
Biltmore Estate Sweet Chardonnay	Soft and honeyed with a fruity background	Pasta dishes, chicken salad
Biltmore Estate Johannisberg Riesling	Floral and spicy with an apricot finish	Fruit, sweet-and-sour dishes, apple pie
Biltmore Estate Chenin Blanc	Overtones of banana and pineapple with a typical varietal character; a lively medium-sweet and fresh wine	Summer fruit desserts
Biltmore Estate Chenin Blanc Special Reserve	Ripe tropical fruit; luscious and flavorful sweet wine	Fresh fruit, berries
Biltmore House White	Fresh and lively; a fruity, medium-sweet wine	Fruit pies, other desserts
ROSÉ WINES		
Biltmore Estate Zinfandel Blanc de Noir	Raspberries and spices in a soft, medium-sweet version	Pâtés, pizza
Biltmore Estate Cabernet Sauvignon Blanc de Noir	Strawberries, peaches, and apricots with a hint of bell peppers in a balanced, medium-sweet wine	Quiches, white meat sandwiches, sausages, chocolate desserts
RED WINES		
Chateau Biltmore Pinot Noir	Spicy cherries with earthy nuances; a balanced and complex wine	Ham, beef stew
Chateau Biltmore Vanderbilt Claret	Lush fruit, smooth and lovely texture; a round and elegant wine	Rack of lamb, quail
Chateau Biltmore Merlot	Red berries with touches of violet and light peppermint in a velvety texture	Poultry, roast
Chateau Biltmore Cabernet Sauvignon	Soft and lush with great little red berries in a smoky background	Red meat, pheasant
Biltmore Estate Cabernet Sauvignon	Lush, balanced wine with black currant and plum flavors and touches of oakiness	Partridge, venison, red meat
Biltmore Estate Cardinal's Crest	Fruity and spicy; a medium-bodied smooth wine	Turkey, chicken, pork roast, rabbit
SPARKLING WINES *Methode Champenoise*		
Chateau Biltmore Brut	Creamy with light hazelnut and mint flavors	Caviar, chicken, leek quiches, crawfish
Biltmore Estate Blanc de Blanc Brut	Creamy, fresh sparkler with lovely balanced flavors	Appetizers in puff pastry, sausages
Biltmore Estate Blanc de Blanc Sec	Sweeter; hints of bread, butter, and honey	Light desserts
Biltmore Estate Rosé Brut	Crisp and lively with tangy raspberry fruit	Leg of lamb, ham

Recipe Index

Acknowledgments & Credits

Biltmore Estate Project Committee:

W. A. V. Cecil

Randy Fluharty

Philippe Jourdain

Diane LeBeau

Roy Jensen

Bernard Delille

Jerry Douglas

Ann Ashley

Jeffry Frank

Liz Calhoun

Julia Weede

Elizabeth Sims

Marla Tambellina

Kelly Simpson

Contributing Photographers:

Courtland Richards: pages 18–19

James Valentine: pages 30–31

Oxmoor House wishes to thank the following merchants and individuals:

Attila, San Francisco, CA

Sara Jane Ball, Birmingham, AL

Biltmore Estate Gift Shops, Asheville, NC

Bridges Antiques, Birmingham, AL

Bromberg's, Mountain Brook, AL

Christine's, Mountain Brook, AL

Frankie Engel Antiques, Birmingham, AL

Ann Gish, Newberry Park, CA

Gorham Inc., Mt. Kisco, NY

Noritake Co., Inc., Port Wentworth, GA